From One Faith Partner to Another

It has been with renewed joy that I have been teaching the Book of the Revelation.

The Letters to the Churches have again enriched my soul. In studying them, I found myself thinking about you Faith Partners, wondering what kind of church experiences you might be passing through. Perhaps some of you are suffering as in Smyrna. There may be those about you who are doctrinally true but who have left their first love. Perhaps others of you are being harassed by false teaching as in Thyatira. Perhaps you find yourself in the midst of an active church but one which God designates as having a name that it lives, yet it is dead. I am sure, however, that each of you personally would come under the promises made to the church in Philadelphia.

God has set an open door before us. We are not many when compared with world population figures. But what a privilege of being united as one for Christ with a wide-open door of ministry before us.

It is with joy that I send you as a 30th ʳʸ remembrance, Volume I of our studies in Re treasure you in our hearts and before God. A we move forward united in faith, God has and untold responsibilities yet for us. We and by faith we venture forth in of opportunity.

Accept our thanks for your par trials, tests and successes. We are united Though scattered over many miles, yet in Him w ear as the members of one body.

Yours for more faith,

Theo H. Epp

Theodore H. Epp

Grace Leavitt

PRACTICAL STUDIES IN

REVELATION

VOLUME I

Christ and the Church

by Theodore H. Epp

Founder and Director
of Back to the Bible Broadcast

$1.50

order from

BACK TO THE BIBLE BROADCAST

Box 233   Lincoln, Nebraska 68501

100,000 printed to date—1969
(5-8891 — 100M — 49)

Printed in the United States of America

Foreword and Dedication

In January 1969, Theodore Epp began a series of radio messages on the Book of the Revelation. These messages were the fruit of Mr. Epp's detailed study of the Bible which has spanned more than 42 years. This accumulated knowledge of the Word is herewith put into more permanent form and made available for distribution.

Practical Studies in Revelation, Volume I, covers the first three chapters of the Book of the Revelation. Chapters 4 through 22 of Revelation will be discussed in Volume II. More space has been given proportionately to the first three chapters because they are considered to be the key to understanding the message of the Book, which is The Victorious Christ.

As suggested by the title, *Practical Studies in Revelation,* the purpose of this study is to relate the truths of this first century book to twentieth century readers. This study is not intended to be an exhaustive commentary on Revelation, but rather it is intended to teach the truths of the Book of the Revelation as they relate to our daily lives.

Because of the differences between speaking and writing, radio messages must be carefully edited and, if necessary, rewritten to make them readable. For nearly 15 years the Rev. John I. Paton was Mr. Epp's personal editorial assistant. Mr. Paton spent many hours laboring over radio messages, preparing them for printed form.

This book, *Practical Studies in Revelation, Volume I,* is the last that Mr. Paton prepared for printed form before his death, when the Lord called him home on March 21, 1969. His heart was so devoted to his work that even after he entered the hospital he was very concerned that this volume be completed. In compliance with his request, the material was taken to him and from his hospital bed he edited the last eight radio messages for this volume.

We have only gratitude to God for this dear brother and for his careful work done unto the Lord. Therefore, we lovingly dedicate this volume to his memory.

–Harold J. Berry
Literature Editor

In Memoriam

Rev. John I. Paton
(1907–1969)

Born in Scotland, March 1, 1907, Mr. Paton came to the United States as a young man. He graduated from Denver (Colo.) Bible Institute in 1929 and later attended Presbyterian Seminary in Omaha, Nebraska, and Dana College in Blair, Nebraska. He taught in Denver Bible Institute and in the National Bible Institute in New York City before accepting a pastorate in Tekamah, Nebraska, in 1936. While a minister in that small town he also served as a part-time instructor at Omaha Baptist Bible Institute. In 1945 he moved to Plymouth, Michigan, where he pastored a church until 1949 when he returned to Omaha Baptist Bible

Institute as a full-time instructor. He joined the Back to the Bible editorial department in 1954.

As Theodore Epp's personal editorial assistant, Mr. Paton adapted the Broadcast director's radio messages for book and magazine publication. As literature editor, he edited all books published by Back to the Bible, and in addition wrote a monthly editorial for the *Good News Broadcaster*, contributed occasional articles to the magazine, and was the editor of the *Faith Partner Bulletin*.

Mr. Paton died on March 21, 1969, from a rare liver disease. The Back to the Bible Broadcast suffered a great loss with his homegoing, for his was a strategic position and was ably filled by his keen theological insight and his admirable Spirit-filled life.

CONTENTS

Chapter One

Can Revelation Be Understood?

Perhaps no Book in the Bible is more misunderstood and misinterpreted than the Book of the Revelation. Many of God's own people say that it is so full of symbolic language, who can understand it?

Some persons interpret the Book as being entirely Jewish. They believe it was fulfilled when Jerusalem fell to the Romans in A.D. 70 and the Israelites left in the land were dispersed among the Gentiles. So the conclusion of those holding this interpretation is that there is nothing in the Book that has any message for us today.

Some others say that the Revelation deals with outstanding events throughout all the Christian era, thus making it more or less a history book for Christians today.

Still others interpret all the Book as listing events associated with the future coming of Christ. According to this interpretation there is really no message for us at the present time, for all is future.

Then there are those who would spiritualize the entire Book. Their position is that the signs and symbols simply reveal the perpetual conflict between good and evil, until good finally wins the victory.

Most Christians, however, seem to be afraid to read and study the Book at all. This is unfortunate. We admit there are difficulties with regard to interpretation. Some of the details and symbolic language are not always easy to understand. Nevertheless, it is a book God has given us and it is an open book, not a closed one. There are elements of truth in some

9

of the interpretations just cited, but the Revelation is not a book sealed with mystery as some have taught. It is open to the heart and mind willing to do the will of God.

The fact is that the very first words in the Book are key words to the understanding of its message and content. As we study it we will find, as others have before us, that the Bible is its own best interpreter.

The opening words are, "The Revelation of Jesus Christ." The key word to the whole content and message of the Book is "Revelation."

First of all, then, it is a revelation. The word "revelation" comes from the Greek word *apokalupsis* which means an uncovering, a disclosure or unveiling. We are familiar with the custom of a sculptor making a statue of some person, or an artist painting a picture, which is later unveiled so that the public can see it.

Just so here. The Bible tells us that what we have in this Book is the unveiling of "Jesus Christ." It is not "The Revelation of Saint John the Divine," as many copies of the Bible entitle the Book. The word "of" in that title means "written by," which of course is true. John was the human author, but the Revelation is not the Revelation of John but of Jesus Christ. That which was previously concealed is now revealed. Even though there are difficulties in understanding or interpreting certain passages in the Book, it was not written to be a mystery but rather to more clearly reveal or unveil certain truths concerning Jesus Christ. So we approach it expecting to learn from it, not expecting to be led into confusion.

This calls for a reading of the Book and a study of it. We will find as we do that God unveils Christ to us, presenting Him as both the Subject and the Object of the Book. It is a revelation of Him who is its Subject, that is, it is given by Him. He is also its Object so it is also about Him. Thus, we have a revelation of Jesus Christ, by Him and about Him.

The word "revelation" conveys the meaning of a spiritual illumination, not an intellectual finding. Science and human knowledge can never grasp or fathom for one single minute the truth as revealed in this glorious Book. All true spiritual knowledge is imparted knowledge, not acquired by the unaided, natural mind of the unsaved man.

The child of God can comprehend this unveiling of Jesus Christ if he desires it. Concerning the need for the illumination of the Holy Spirit in understanding the Scriptures the Apostle Paul wrote: "But as it is written, Eye hath not seen, nor ear heard, neither have entered into the heart of man, the things which God hath prepared for them that love him [the unsaved man does not understand what God has prepared for those who are born again]. But God hath revealed them unto us by his Spirit: for the Spirit searcheth all things, yea, the deep things of God. For what man knoweth the things of a man, save the spirit of man which is in him? even so the things of God knoweth no man, but the Spirit of God [this is a basic truth]. Now we have received, not the spirit of the world, but the Spirit which is of God; that we might know the things that are freely given to us of God. Which things also we speak, not in the words which man's wisdom teacheth, but which the Holy Ghost teacheth; comparing spiritual things with spiritual. But the natural man [the man who is not born again, or the Christian who is trying to understand spiritual truth on a natural basis] receiveth not the things of the Spirit of God: for they are foolishness unto him: neither can he know them, because they are spiritually discerned" (I Cor. 2:9-14).

This same truth is repeated in Ephesians where Paul, in praying for believers, says, "That the God of our Lord Jesus Christ, the Father of glory, may give unto you the Spirit of wisdom and revelation [illumination] in the knowledge of him: the eyes of your understanding [the inner spiritual eyes] being enlightened; that ye may know [understand] what is the hope of his calling, and what the riches of the glory of his inheritance in the saints" (1:17,18). The Spirit of God, as part of His divine work for believers, opens the Bible to our understanding as we depend upon Him.

So then, the Book of the Revelation is the unveiling of Jesus Christ. It gives us final truth about Him. This is truth given by God to Him which He then passed on through John to us.

This is the way we receive it. God gave the truth to Christ. While He was in the flesh on earth, He had only partial knowledge of the prophetic timetable. We are speaking here of the manward side of Jesus, not the side of His deity. He said in Mark 13:32, "But of that day and that hour knoweth no man, no, not the angels which are in heaven, neither the Son, but the Father."

After the resurrection there was a difference. In speaking to His disciples in His resurrected, glorified body He said, when they asked Him if He would at this time restore again the kingdom to Israel: "It is not for you to know the times or the season, which the Father hath put in his own power." The indication here is that the Saviour knew the answer to this question but still was not disclosing it. As the God-man at the right hand of the Father He knows all things.

The Book we are studying is "the Revelation of Jesus Christ, which God [the Father] gave unto him." Jesus Christ in His preexistent state was eternally God. Being God He created all things and for Him all things exist. This is clearly presented in Colossians 1:15-18: "Who is the image of the invisible God, the firstborn of every creature: for by him were all things created, that are in heaven, and that are in earth, visible and invisible, whether they be thrones, or dominions, or principalities, or powers: all things were created by him, and for him: And he is before all things, and by him all things consist. And he is the head of the body, the church: who is the beginning, the firstborn from the dead; that in all things he might have the preeminence."

The Lord Jesus did not cease being a member of the Godhead when He took on human flesh and came to this earth to redeem us. He did, however, lay aside some of His glory temporarily, a glory which He prayed would be restored to Him after His redemptive work was over. He said in John 17:5, "And now, O Father, glorify thou me with thine own self with the glory which I had with thee before the world was." He veiled off much of that glory while here among men. He did not, during the days of His ministry, exercise all the privileges that belonged to Him as a member of the Godhead. But these privileges were restored at His resurrection and ascension. So there were things that Jesus as man, while He dwelt on earth, did not know; though He knew them in His preexistent state and now knows them again since He is One with the Father.

If after studying this Book of the Revelation, the Lord Jesus Christ does not mean more to you than He did before, either I have failed in teaching it, or the Holy Spirit has not been able to reveal this glorious truth to you. The unveiling of Jesus Christ is the central content of the Book.

Chapter Two

Some Basic Matters
(Rev. 1:1-3)

The Person of Christ

Three outstanding facts about Christ are revealed to us in the Book of the Revelation. First is His Person, second is His power, and third is His ultimate program.

First of all there is the unveiling of the Person of Jesus Christ. He is identified as the "Alpha and Omega, the beginning and the ending . . . which is, and which was, and which is to come, the Almighty" (Rev. 1:8). He is described here as the absolute, final Word. He is Deity. There is nothing before Him or after Him, and nothing above or beneath Him.

John states in his Gospel: "In the beginning was the Word [Christ], and the Word was with God, and the Word was God. The same was in the beginning with God. All things were made by him; and without him was not any thing made that was made" (1:1-3). This tells us about Christ's place in that beginning. Then we read in verse 14: "And the Word was made flesh, and dwelt among us." Of course this refers to His first coming when He took on the form of a man in order to be our Redeemer.

The revelation of His Person as He is today is given in Revelation, chapter 1. This we will consider in more detail later.

He is the ultimate end of all things, and concerning this we read in Revelation 21:3-6: "And I heard a great voice out of heaven saying, Behold, the tabernacle of God is with men, and he will dwell with them, and they shall be his people, and

God himself shall be with them, and be their God. And God shall wipe away all tears from their eyes; and there shall be no more death, neither sorrow, nor crying, neither shall there be any more pain: for the former things are passed away. And he that sat upon the throne said, Behold, I make all things new. And he said unto me, Write: for these words are true and faithful. And he said unto me, It is done. I am Alpha and Omega, the beginning and the end. I will give unto him that is athirst of the fountain of the water of life freely."

This great passage is brought to a close in Revelation 22:12,13: "And, behold, I come quickly; and my reward is with me, to give every man according as his work shall be. I am Alpha and Omega, the beginning and the end, the first and the last."

The Power of Christ

There is also the unveiling of the power of Jesus Christ. First we see His personal power over all creatures, beasts, rulers, angels, man, and Satan. All are subject to Christ's personal power. None can escape Him, whether it is for judgment or to be employed in some useful purpose.

We also find His instrumental power is revealed in this Book of the Revelation. That is, He has at His disposal and makes use of all the elements such as earthquakes, lightning, thunder, light, hail, rain, forces of the air and all kinds of plagues. He calls into use all spiritual beings such as angels whether they are good or evil. He even makes use of Satan to bring judgment upon the earth. The Lord Jesus Christ uses all His power either for destructive judgment or for constructive purposes, whichever He knows is best. He is the final word in all things.

The Purpose of Christ

There is also the unveiling of His purpose and program. First of all, He has an ultimate purpose, and second, He has a progressive program.

The ultimate purpose of God is to dwell with man. Man is to be blessed in God, and God is to be glorified in man. John in his Gospel points to this goal: "He came unto his own [things], and his own [people] received him not. But as many as received him, to them gave he power to become the sons of God, even to them that believe on his name: Which were born, not of blood, nor of the will of the flesh, nor of the will of man, but of God. And the Word [Christ] was made flesh, and dwelt among us, (and we beheld his glory, the glory as of the only begotten of the Father,) full of grace and truth" (1:11-14).

Though God's ultimate purpose was not realized in Christ's first coming, it will be fulfilled eventually. In the Revelation John writes: "And I John saw the holy city, new Jerusalem, coming down from God out of heaven, prepared as a bride adorned for her husband. And I heard a great voice out of heaven saying, Behold, the tabernacle of God is with men, and he will dwell with them, and they shall be his people, and God himself shall be with them, and be their God" (21:2,3). Then it is that the ultimate purpose of God will be fulfilled. We can say, "Hallelujah!" to that. So much for the ultimate purpose of God.

Now consider His progressive program, the work He is doing now and will continue to do until He completes it. Presently He is at war with sin and will eventually destroy it. He will never make peace with it. The world is trying to coexist with sin, and some Christians in their worldliness try to do the same. But no Christian can really coexist with sin. Christ Jesus came to destroy sin, and He does this in our lives now. He is pictured to us in the Revelation as having a drawn sword, fighting sin to the finish.

In Psalm 46 we read this wonderful passage: "God is our refuge and strength, a very present help in trouble. Therefore will not we fear, though the earth be removed, and though the mountains be carried into the midst of the sea; though the waters thereof roar and be troubled, though the mountains shake with the swelling thereof" (vv. 1-3). We shall not fear because the Lord is in control and is working to destroy sin.

Thus we are introduced to the unveiling of Jesus Christ in His Person in Revelation, chapter 1. There we also see His glory as He is today. In chapters 2 and 3 we see Him unveiled in His relationship to the Church as His grace is unfolded toward the Church, His bride. Then we see Him unveiled in the processes through which He sets up His kingdom (chapters 4-22). The consummation of His plans for the government of the world are clearly set forth.

Christ's Willing Bondslaves

Turning again to Revelation 1:1 we have these words: "The Revelation of Jesus Christ, which God gave unto him, to shew unto his servants things which must shortly come to pass." The expression "to shew" means to show by making known. The Lord will make known to His servants things that soon will come to pass. The word "servant" means "bondman" or "slave" and has reference not to someone enslaved against his will but to born-again believers who are freewill bondmen to Christ. They have surrendered their own rights to the Lord, gladly submitting to His rulership, not wanting to run their own lives. It is to such the Book of the Revelation will be made plain.

If you are in that category you will receive great spiritual help from this Book. If, on the other hand, you are a wayward Christian, if you are not living a Christian life as you should, you may indeed be frightened by some things stated in this last book in the Bible. At the same time it may be for your good to be exercised by such facts so that you surrender your all to Him.

If you are outside of the fold, if you have never been born again, even though you may be a church member, may even be considered religious, you need to consider where you stand with relation to these things. If you have never taken Jesus Christ as your personal Lord and Saviour so that your sin and guilt have been removed, then all you can look forward to is the judgment clearly set forth in the Revelation.

The expression "shortly come to pass" means "will come to pass quickly and with certainty." God's program is all set. No amount of interference by men or governments of men will ever alter God's program. Many people are fearful of the present scientific experiments which some declare will destroy all life on this earth. The danger is that our fear of what man can do may make us overlook what the Bible predicts God will do in judgment during the Tribulation. Men have made great strides in scientific achievements, some good and some bad; but when the best of these are compared with God's work, they are very small indeed. Furthermore, man could not do what he is doing in the way of science if he were not obeying God's arranged order. The satellites man sends up into space have to overcome gravity, but only to a certain degree or they would fly out of control into outer space. To be of any use they have to fit in with God's established physical laws.

When we compare man's scientific achievements with God's handiwork, man's accomplishments look, and are, very small. Putting satellites into orbit around the earth is a remarkable achievement by man, but what are these compared to the moon or the stars in their orbits?

Men have made great advances from the time they built the tower of Babel. They now erect huge skyscrapers in many of our cities that dwarf Babel's tower. For long centuries man depended upon wind or manpower to propel his ships. Now that we live in the atomic age we witness almost unbelievable advances. Man is able to take a certain amount of matter, about the size of a golf ball, and operate a submarine on it for two years. Power is derived from the atom through controlling its energy and heat. But since the creation God has been producing energy and heat from matter for the whole universe, not only for the world we live in.

Our earth is but a tiny speck compared to most heavenly bodies, but we are dependent upon God's atomic sun for heat and light. For the purpose of producing energy and heat,

4,620,000 tons of material are burned every second. An atomic bomb exploded by men may be visible for a few hundred miles. But the atomic energy from the sun produces and radiates continuous light from the sun to the earth, a distance of some 93 million miles.

Tremendous heat is generated by atomic explosions but that is dissipated within a few miles. Yet, though we live some 93 million miles from the sun, its heat would be unbearable if God had not protected us by an atmosphere provided for that pupose, though not for that alone.

Some of the satellites men are sending into the stratosphere weigh as much as several tons. When we look at the earth, which is one of the smallest of the planets God has made, we find, according to scientists, that it weighs six trillion, six hundred quintrillion tons. In figures this would be 66 plus 20 zeros.

This world of ours orbits around the sun according to the plan of God. Man has put his little moons into orbit around the earth, but he has to obey God's order of things to do it. One of these we call the law of gravity. The Russian Communists, who are atheists, say there isn't any God; but they could not launch a single satellite if they ignored what men so often call the laws of nature. Though the Russians refuse to acknowledge God, they still must send their satellites up into the stratosphere at a certain distance from the earth, and to keep it there it must travel at a certain speed. If it moves, let's say at 10,000 miles an hour, it would be drawn back to the earth. If it travels at 25,000 miles an hour it will fly out into space. Through his experimentations man has learned some of what can be done and what cannot be done in outer space.

We know that if you tie a ball to a string and start whirling the ball around it will remain in a kind of orbit around your finger, provided you keep the ball moving at a high enough speed. This is akin to what man has found out with regard to satellites and the law of gravity.

Yet how small are man's accomplishments in this area compared with the motions of the moon, the earth and the sun. The moon is some 240,000 miles away and weighs 80 quintrillion tons, which is about 8 plus 19 zeros. The diameter of the moon is some 2160 miles, and it travels at the rate of 2300 miles per hour. It orbits the earth in a certain prescribed manner, and the moon and the earth together travel around the sun.

Should the power of gravity be suspended for a single second, everything on the surface of the earth would fly off into space. We would have the greatest catastrophe the universe has ever known.

What I am seeking to point out here is that God is in control of all things. We should be thankful for what men are learning concerning God's universe and how it operates and what is the source of power and energy that we depend upon. All this information emphasizes, to those who are willing to see, how great God is and that all things are in His hands.

We have the record in the Scripture that at one time God made "the sun stand still." Scientists, even devout scientists, may try to explain how this could be done, but whether or not we know how God did it, we know He did it during the early days of Israel's conquest of Canaan.

If we are going to be afraid in these days, let us be afraid in an area that really counts. It is better to be afraid of God's judgments, remembering that He can destroy both body and soul in hell. He has made provision for men's salvation through faith in Jesus Christ. If they reject Him, they die without hope; if they receive Him, they will be saved for all eternity. This is what God can do for you in the spiritual realm.

Men are willfully blind if they do not see the handiwork of God around them. Paul wrote in Romans, chapter 1: "For the invisible things of him from the creation of the world are clearly seen, being understood by the things that are made, even his eternal power and Godhead; so that they are without excuse: Because that, when they knew God, they glorified him not as God, neither were thankful; but became vain in their imaginations, and their foolish heart was darkened. Professing themselves to be wise, they became fools, And changed the glory of the uncorruptible God into an image made like to corruptible man, and to birds, and fourfooted beasts, and creeping things. Wherefore God also gave them up to uncleanness through the lusts of their own hearts, to dishonour their own bodies between themselves: Who changed the truth of God into a lie, and worshipped and served the creature more than the Creator, who is blessed for ever. Amen" (vv. 20-25).

God will manifest His power again in remarkable works and these will be among the events which the Book of the Revelation says must shortly come to pass. Some of these startling events are described in Matthew 24:27-30: "For as the lightning cometh out of the east, and shineth even unto the west; so shall also the coming of the Son of man be. For wheresoever the carcase is, there will the eagles be gathered together. Immediately after the tribulation of those days shall the sun be darkened, and the moon shall not give her light, and the stars shall fall from heaven, and the powers of the heavens shall be shaken: And then shall appear the sign of the Son of man in heaven: and then shall all the tribes of the earth mourn, and they shall see the Son of man coming in the clouds of heaven with power and great glory."

Luke in his Gospel tells us the same things in these words: "And there shall be signs in the sun, and in the moon, and in the stars; and upon the earth distress of nations, with perplexity; the sea and the waves roaring; men's hearts failing them for fear, and for looking after those things which are coming on the earth: for the powers of heaven shall be shaken. And then shall they see the Son of man coming in a cloud with power and great glory. And when these things begin to come to pass, then look up, and lift up your heads; for your redemption draweth nigh" (21:25-28). These events should not terrify the people of God on the earth but cause them to look up, knowing that the coming of the Lord is near.

Peter also tells us of some of the changes that will come when God displays His power afresh: "But the day of the Lord will come as a thief in the night; in the which the heavens shall pass away with a great noise, and the elements shall melt with fervent heat, the earth also and the works that are therein shall be burned up. Seeing then that all these things shall be dissolved, what manner of persons ought ye to be in all holy conversation and godliness, Looking for and hasting unto the coming of the day of God, wherein the heavens being on fire shall be dissolved, and the elements shall melt with fervent heat? Nevertheless we, according to his promise, look for new heavens and a new earth, wherein dwelleth righteousness. Wherefore, beloved, seeing that ye look for such things, be diligent that ye may be found of him in peace, without spot, and blameless. And account that the longsuffering of our Lord is salvation" (II Pet. 3:10-15).

A strong warning is also contained in Hebrews 12: "See that ye refuse not him that speaketh. For if they escaped not who refused him that spake on earth, much more shall not we escape, if we turn away from him that speaketh from heaven: Whose voice then shook the earth: but now he hath promised, saying, Yet once more I shake not the earth only, but also heaven. And this word, Yet once more, signifieth the removing of those things that are shaken, as of things that are made, that those things which cannot be shaken may remain" (vv. 25-27).

This is a very important passage of Scripture. The very things that men depend upon so much—the material things of the earth—shall be burned up and dissolved so that things which cannot be shaken will remain.

Those who know the Lord Jesus have this promise: "Wherefore we receiving a kingdom which cannot be moved, let us have grace, whereby we may serve God acceptably with reverence and godly fear" (Heb. 12:28). We who know the Lord Jesus Christ as our Saviour can rest with assurance in God's promises and the knowledge of His love. In Romans 8 the question is asked, "Who shall separate us from the love of Christ?" And then follows one of the most remarkable passages in Scripture asserting our safety in Christ and assuring us that nothing can separate us from His love. The glorious hope of the Church of this age is that its members will be snatched away from this earth into the presence of the Lord before all these great earthshaking events take place. No one is able to pluck us out of the Father's hands or shake us out of His hands. If you are trusting in Christ as personal Saviour, you are in the hands of God.

A Threefold Beatitude

Verse 3 of Revelation 1 contains a threefold beatitude. The verse reads: "Blessed is he that readeth, and they that hear the words of this prophecy, and keep those things which are written therein: for the time is at hand."

A blessing is promised, first of all, to those who read the Book of the Revelation. Some may have bypassed this Book because they find it full of figures and symbols they do not understand, and what they do understand makes them afraid. The promise of God is that we will be blessed if we read it. This is an age that counts much on happiness, but true happiness to the Christian lies in following the directions of the Lord.

And this is also a promise to those who hear the words of this Book. This would have reference to listening to others reading it or us making it our own. This would include studying it and remembering what we find in it.

The third aspect of this beatitude has to do with those who "keep those things which are written therein." God does not ask us to read the Book of the Revelation so that we might speculate concerning future events. It does not mean reading it in order to satisfy our curiosity concerning God's future program. If we read it with the purpose of discovering the principles of life which God has revealed in it, and determine by His grace to conform to these principles, then we will indeed be blessed.

There is an urgency expressed in this verse also with regard to such obedience. We are told here that the time of the fulfillment of these events is close at hand. This is in line with Peter's admonition in II Peter 3:11-13: "Seeing then that all these things shall be dissolved, what manner of

persons ought ye to be in all holy conversation and godliness,
Looking for and hasting unto the coming of the day of God,
wherein the heavens being on fire shall be dissolved, and the
elements shall melt with fervent heat? Nevertheless we,
according to his promise, look for new heavens and a new
earth, wherein dwelleth righteousness." Are we looking
forward to the bringing of righteousness to the world? Is this
the joy of our hearts? If so, heed what Peter further says in
verse 14: "Seeing that ye look for such things, be diligent
that ye may be found of him in peace, without spot, and
blameless." The very movement of world events should stir
us up to be ready at any moment for Christ's coming.

But some will object and say that these Scriptures were
given a long time ago and Christ has not come yet. The
reason is given in verse 15 of II Peter 3: "And account that
the longsuffering of our Lord is salvation." He has held off in
order to give men a chance to be saved. He is not willing that
any should perish. The events spoken of are judgment events
and God does not want to bring such on the earth without
giving men more than an adequate opportunity to repent of
their sins.

We see from the above that the Book of the Revelation
was not written for speculation but for heart preparation on
the part of God's people.

Chapter Three

A Word of Greeting
(Rev. 1:4-8)

This section tells who the human author is, some of those to whom he is writing, and the basic things he wants them to understand. Part of the passage is as follows: "John to the seven churches which are in Asia: Grace be unto you, and peace, from him which is, and which was, and which is to come; and from the seven Spirits which are before his throne; And from Jesus Christ, who is the faithful witness, and the first begotten of the dead, and the prince of the kings of the earth. Unto him that loved us, and washed us from our sins in his own blood, And hath made us kings and priests unto God and his Father; to him be glory and dominion for ever and ever" (vv. 4-6).

The seven churches of Asia are dealt with at length in chapters 2 and 3 which we will consider later. However, in the greeting sent to the churches, John wished them grace and peace from the Lord. In the portion dealing with the Lord Jesus Christ, glory and dominion are ascribed to Him.

We are inclined to pass over such phrases as "grace and peace" and "glory and dominion" as though they were mere formalities of expression. They are far more than that. There is depth of meaning in them that is worth investigating.

With regard to grace we find that it is a gift without any strings attached. So the salutation or greeting to the churches is that there is a gift for them for their asking and receiving. In fact, there is more than one gift. It is many gifts. With the gift of life God adds much else.

25

The word "peace" signifies that a war that has previously existed has ceased. The unsaved person is in a hopeless war against God. Such a person may be under conviction, but unless he accepts God's offer of peace the warfare will continue through this life and into eternity. God's peace is made through Jesus Christ. Peace must be made on God's terms which are very clearly set forth in the Scriptures.

Paul speaks of "repentance toward God, and faith toward our Lord Jesus Christ." The word "repentance" means a change of mind which leads to a change of heart. Many of us think of God as sitting high on a throne, full of love, and up to that point we are right. But then many argue that God will never judge any of his creatures regardless of how much they resist Him or rebel against Him and reject His way of salvation. This is a wrong view of God. We will have to change our minds about Almighty God who sent His own Son to die in order that you and I might live. So there must be repentance toward God and faith toward our Lord Jesus Christ.

Christ is the One who suffered in our place, and our faith must be placed in Him. Such faith is not a mere historical belief that He existed. As we truly accept Him as our Saviour we first repent or change our minds with regard to God. The Apostle Paul tells us in Romans 5:10: "For if, when we were enemies, we were reconciled to God by the death of his Son, much more, being reconciled, we shall be saved by his life."

Source of the Salutation

We are next told in this salutation the source of this grace and peace. It is "from him which is, and which was, and which is to come; and from the seven Spirits which are before his throne; And from Jesus Christ, who is the faithful witness."

The expression "him which is, and which was, and which is to come," will include the Father and also the Son, for the Lord Jesus is God. We read in the Gospel of John: "In the beginning was the Word, and the Word was with God, and the

Word was God. The same was in the beginning with God. All things were made by him; and without him was not any thing made that was made" (vv. 1-3). Then we learn in verse 14 how Christ was made flesh and dwelt among us and we beheld his glory, the glory as of the only begotten of the Father, full of grace and truth.

This is brought to us from another angle in Hebrews 1:1-3: "God, who at sundry times and in divers manners spake in time past unto the fathers by the prophets, Hath in these last days spoken unto us by his Son, whom he hath appointed heir of all things, by whom also he made the worlds; Who being the brightness of his glory, and the express image of his person, and upholding all things by the word of his power, when he had by himself purged our sins, sat down on the right hand of the Majesty on high." The greeting then is from the Godhead who dwells in all eternity.

In Exodus 3:14 where the Lord is first introduced as Jehovah of the Old Testament, He is revealed as the Becoming One. So in the three tenses of the verb to be, we have God described as the God of all eternity past, the God of the present time, and the God of time in endless future. He has neither beginning nor end. What we know of Him in the past, He will become to us now. And what He does for us now and is to us now, He will always be to us in the endless future. This is the wonderful God from whom this peace is expressed. He is the immutable or unchangeable One who is the same yesterday, today and forever. He, Himself sums this truth up for us in these words: "I am the Lord, I change not" (Mal. 3:6).

This title which speaks of Him as the One who comes, is also a Jewish title for the Messiah. So for both Gentile and Jew He is the Coming One. He is the Messiah of Israel, the Redeemer of His people and the One who greets His own with both grace and peace.

The Spirit of God

The greeting is also from the seven Spirits which are before God's throne. The passage should be understood as the Holy Spirit in all His completeness and perfection before God. He is the Executive Director of the works of God in behalf of man. He is the Divine Administrator. What God the Father and God the Son purpose and plan, God the Holy Spirit will bring to pass. He is the One who is the Helper alongside the believer, the One whom Jesus said He would send in His place.

"Seven" speaks of perfection. In this case it is spiritual perfection.

The word "seven" is used 54 times in the Book of the Revelation. Another significant number is the number "three," which speaks of the Triune God—Father, Son and Holy Spirit. The number three also carries the thought of perfection.

The Holy Spirit's administration of the will of the Father and the Son is perfect and complete. We also find that when Christ was on earth He was empowered by the same "sevenfold Spirit." We read in Isaiah 11:2: "And the spirit of the Lord shall rest upon him [Christ], the spirit of wisdom [Christ had the wisdom given by the Holy Spirit] and understanding [we cannot understand of ourselves but He helps us understand], the spirit of counsel [He will counsel us so that we can help others] and might [the power of deity in Christ who is our power], the spirit of knowledge [knowing and understanding the things of God] and the fear of the Lord [through Him we learn to reverence the Lord]." The Spirit in all His perfection is now at work in the Church of Jesus Christ. He is also at work in each individual believer. We read in I Corinthians 12: "Now there are diversities of gifts, but the same Spirit. And there are differences of administrations, but the same Lord. And there are diversities of operations, but it is the same God which worketh all in all. But the manifestation of the Spirit is given to every man to profit withal. For to one is given by the Spirit the word of wisdom; to another the word of knowledge by the same Spirit; to another faith by the same Spirit" (vv. 4-9). Thus God in His gracious kindness and infinite wisdom works in and through each individual believer through the Holy Spirit who also was in Christ.

Christ's Three Titles

God's message to the Churches came through John the Apostle from the Holy Spirit and from Jesus Christ "who is the faithful witness, and the first begotten of the dead, and the prince of the kings of the earth. Unto him that loved us, and washed us from our sins in his own blood, And hath made us kings and priests unto God and his Father" (Rev. 1:5,6).

We have here a fivefold statement in which Christ is given three titles. First He is called a "faithful witness," because He is a Prophet. Second, He is called the "first begotten of the dead," for He is Priest. Third, He is named "the prince [leader] of the kings of the earth," so He is also King.

Jesus Christ, the Faithful Witness

The word "witness" comes from the same Greek word as does the word "martyr." This especially fits Christ for He was a witness even unto death. During His public ministry He was faithful in repeating to men the words the Heavenly Father had given Him to speak. These words, whether of judgment or of atonement or of love—whatever the subject—He was faithful in repeating to men.

We have that Word and it is final. Heaven and earth will pass away but the Word of God will not pass away, not even a jot or tittle until all that God has said will be fulfilled.

When Jesus Christ gave His message He was speaking as Creator of all things and Controller of all things and the One who has all the past, the present and the future in His hands. He is eternal and will stand as the witness of God when all man-made things have come to nothing.

He has given us the truth concerning the condemnation of the unbeliever. Any who refuse to listen to Him concerning salvation will have no excuse. His Word is clear and plain. There is no way of being saved except through Him.

He revealed the love of God when He stated, "For God so loved the world [humanity], that he gave his only begotten Son, that whosoever believeth in him should not perish, but have everlasting life." He not only proclaimed that love but He also expressed it by dying as a substitute for all men. We learn that it was "while we were yet sinners, Christ died for us."

He is the faithful witness of God's intent and purposes concerning the world of men. It is not God's desire to condemn the world and thus destroy men but rather to save them. Christ came according to Luke 19:10 "to seek and to save that which was lost." What we need to do is believe His word.

He is a faithful witness concerning God's pleasure and displeasure. We read in Psalm 116:15: "Precious in the sight of the Lord is the death of his saints." How can the death of one who is born again bring pleasure to God? The reason is that because of the redemption in Christ Jesus, a believer, when he dies, is ushered into God's presence.

Over against that God says He has no pleasure in the death of the wicked. God is not a tyrant making it hard for any man to get to heaven. He has done everything possible for man to be saved and to live in God's presence forever. When a man rejects Christ, it is God's heart that is broken. He has no pleasure in the death of Christ rejectors. In the light of the provision God has made for man's salvation, those who reject His offer bear the responsibility for their own eternal loss.

The Lord Jesus Christ has been a faithful witness concerning the righteousness of God. He has declared God's righteousness showing how He is just and the Justifier of him who believes in Jesus. It is this very characteristic of God that makes it impossible for Him to allow sin in heaven or even the thought of it. Atonement was made for sin through Christ. So all who trust Him, all who dare to believe in Him are justified and are given eternal life.

Our Lord was faithful in His witness even unto death. In Pilate's judgment hall Christ did not deny that He was the Son of God. He affirmed it. He could not and would not deny the truth concerning Himself. Though He might have been spared some suffering and scorn, He did not hesitate to witness before Pilate and the High Priest of Israel concerning Himself and God's purposes through Him.

He was also a faithful witness concerning the individuals who refuse to believe. All judgment is given into the hands of the Son. Concerning the last great judgment of unbelievers the Word says, "And I saw the dead, small and great, stand before God; and the books were opened: and another book was opened, which is the book of life: and the dead were judged out of those things which were written in the books, according to their works. And the sea gave up the dead which were in it; and death and hell delivered up the dead which were in them: and they were judged every man according to their works. And death and hell were cast into the lake of fire. This is the second death. And whosoever was not found written in the book of life was cast into the lake of fire" (Rev. 20:12-15). Christ is a faithful witness for He has not hesitated to tell men of the dangers of the lake of fire.

Christ is also a faithful witness in telling the believer that there is yet a judgment ahead for the child of God. This is not a judgment with regard to salvation but one concerning our works whether they have been good or bad. The Lord says in this Book of the Revelation, "Behold, I come quickly; and my reward is with me, to give every man according as his work shall be (22:12).

So there is a day coming when the words that Jesus spoke while ministering here on the earth, and the life He lived and the death He died, will witness against those who reject Him. And we who are children of God who enjoy the privilege of having the full life of the risen Christ within us, will be tested with regard to the works we did following our salvation.

Our Priest

Christ is not only the Witness or Prophet, He is also the first begotten from the dead, and as such is our Priest. We read of others in the Bible who were brought back to life, that is physical life, only to die again. Christ was the first, and so far the only one, to enter into this new indestructible life. He was raised from the dead in a body that will never see death. He is alive forever. In describing Himself to John He says, "I am he that liveth, and was dead; and, behold, I am alive for evermore."

It is wonderful indeed to know that death will have no more dominion over Him. He died once for all, but now He has been raised once for all (Rom. 6:10). He is the first to enter into this indestructible life and has provided the same kind of life for everyone who will receive Him.

As the first begotten of the Father, Christ has the birthright belonging to that position. This means spiritual blessings far beyond our understanding, and a double portion of them at that.

We read of His spiritual birthright in Philippians 2:7-11: He "made himself of no reputation, and took upon him the form of a servant, and was made in the likeness of men: And being found in fashion as a man, he humbled himself, and became obedient unto death, even the death of the cross. Wherefore God also hath highly exalted him, and given him a name which is above every name: That at the name of Jesus every knee should bow, of things in heaven, and things in earth, and things under the earth; and that every tongue should confess that Jesus Christ is Lord, to the glory of God the Father."

If you are a child of God, you will gladly bow your knee before Him. If you are not a child of God, the day will come when you will have to acknowledge that God has raised Christ from the dead and set Him above all principalities and powers. At that time you will have to bow to Him, and your tongue will confess that Jesus Christ is Lord to the glory of the Father.

Not only does our Lord have the spiritual birthright from God, but the Word tells us we are fellow heirs with Him. We inherit with Him. In a spiritual sense we have also received Him as our life and live in His life. We have been raised together with Him and are made fellow heirs with Him (Rom. 8:17). A day is coming when we will even sit on the right hand of the throne on high together with Him (Rev. 3:21). Even now He has given us the privilege to be in Him and His power is in us to overcome anything that would hem us in or cause us to fall. There is nothing that can conquer us if we by faith take our place with Him, having Him as our spiritual life.

Our King

In the third place the Lord Jesus Christ is called the prince of the rulers of the kings of the earth. This means that He directs the affairs and destinies of men and of nations. Long years ago Nebuchadnezzar learned through God's discipline that the Most High rules in the kingdoms of men and gives power to whomsoever He will. Sometimes the Lord sets over a people the basest of men in order to carry out His program.

Earthly rulers may take it upon themselves to try to crush the Church out of existence, but Christ is King of kings and Lord of lords. Human leaders may have political power over the lives of individual Christians, but these men do not have the final power that belongs to Christ. One of these days He will come again and rule in the position that is rightfully His.

At the present time Satan is the usurper of world rulership. His power is temporary, however, as the ruler of darkness. He does not have final say. Christ is in control and even uses Satan to achieve certain predetermined objectives God Himself has set. The Evil One is limited in his power and actions.

There are times when God uses Satan in the lives of believers just as he was permitted to sift Job. Our God who makes the wrath of man to praise Him can turn the rebellions of Satan to a use that will further serve His divine cause and purposes. We learn in chapter 20 of Revelation that the Evil One will be cast into the bottomless pit for a thousand years but after that will be loosed from his prison for a little season. He will go out to deceive the nations and will succeed in gathering to himself those persons who have not really yielded themselves to God during Christ's reign. Satan will not succeed in overthrowing God but will be used to show who are the true and the false in the millennial earth.

The wicked rebellion against God and His Christ which started at the tower of Babel continues in our day, but Christ will establish His order in His own time. He is indeed ruler of the kings of the earth.

That Jesus Christ is King is stated time and again in the Scriptures. One of the outstanding passages on this subject is Psalm 2. It is a prophetic Psalm covering both the First and Second Comings of Christ. In it there is a very special message for our day. The psalmist raises a question, then tells what the nations are saying: "Why do the nations assemble with commotion, uproar and confusion of voices, and why do the people imagine, meditate upon and devise an empty scheme? The kings of the earth take their places; the rulers are met by appointment, and take counsel against the Lord and His Anointed One—the Messiah, the Christ. They say, [Acts 4:25-27] Let us break Their bands (of restraint) asunder, and cast Their cords [of control] from us" (vv. 1-3, *Amp.*).

Man is not left to his own devices. God speaks: "He Who sits in the heavens laughs; the Lord has them in supreme contempt, and in derision He mocks them. He speaks to them in His deep anger, and troubles, terrifies and confounds them in His displeasure and fury, saying, Yet have I anointed, installed and placed My King firmly on My holy hill of Zion" (vv. 4-6, *Amp.*).

The word "laugh" is not used in this context in the sense we ordinarily think of it. God does not consider man's rebellion something amusing. God holds man's vain boasting

in contempt. Plots of men and nations against the Lord's
Christ are not overlooked but these plots are brought to
nothing, for God will consummate His own purposes. In spite
of all that the nations of the earth can do, the Lord is still the
Alpha and Omega. So the things He began He will finish. In
His own set time He will set Christ upon the throne of the
world.

God's purposes through His Son are stated in verses 7-9.
"I will declare the decree of the Lord: He said to Me, You are
My Son; this day [I declare] I have begotten You. Ask of Me,
and I will give You the nations as Your inheritance, and the
uttermost parts of the earth for Your possession. You shall
break them with a rod of iron; You shall dash them in pieces
like potter's ware" (*Amp.*). This is God's program for the
future and nothing man can do can change it.

Just as in other portions of Scripture where God warns of
judgment to come, He also provides a message of grace. This
Psalm is no exception. God speaks in love and says, "Now
therefore, O you kings, act wisely; be instructed and warned,
O you rulers of the earth. Serve the Lord with reverent awe
and worshipful fear; rejoice and be in high spirits, with
trembling [lest you displease Him]. Kiss the Son—pay
homage to Him in purity—lest He be angry, and you perish in
the way, for soon shall His wrath be kindled. O
blessed—happy, fortunate and to be envied—are all those who
seek refuge and put their trust in Him!" (vv. 10-12, *Amp.*).
What is your response as you read these words from God's
Word?

Peter warns that in the latter days there will be many
persons, wise in their own conceits, who will think they
know more than God. The Lord's statement concerning this
through Peter is, "Knowing this first, that there shall come in
the last days scoffers, walking after their own lusts, And
saying, Where is the promise of his coming? for since the
fathers fell asleep, all things continue as they were from the
beginning of the creation" (II Pet. 3:3,4). This is willfull
ignorance on the part of these persons. Peter charges them
with this, saying, "For this they willingly are ignorant of,

that by the word of God the heavens were of old, and the earth standing out of the water and in the water: Whereby the world that then was, being overflowed with water, perished" (vv. 5,6). Back in Noah's day there were also scoffers who would not believe the message God sent through him. Then the flood came and took them all away.

This further warning is given in verse 7: "The heavens and the earth, which are now, by the same word are kept in store, reserved unto fire against the day of judgment and perdition of ungodly men." Men have their atomic bombs but the greatest atomic bomb of all is the earth itself. It is stored with fire until the day set by God for it to explode.

Once again there is a message of grace with the warning of judgment. There is no need for any person to stay in unbelief. Peter writes, "But, beloved, be not ignorant of this one thing, that one day is with the Lord as a thousand years, and a thousand years as one day. The Lord is not slack concerning his promise, as some men count slackness; but is longsuffering to us-ward, not willing that any should perish, but that all should come to repentance" (vv. 8,9). Time is an element with us but not with God. Just because several thousand years have elapsed since Noah's flood does not mean that God will never judge the earth again. He will do what He says. Time means nothing to Him, for He speaks from the standpoint of eternity. The only reason God withholds judgment now is that men might come to Christ and be saved.

Coming back again to the Book of the Revelation, we find that it is a Book designed to unveil Christ as the rightful Prince of the earth, the Ruler of the earth, the King of kings and Lord of lords. What God predicts will take place will be fulfilled as He states. Christ will one of these days take His rightful place and the world will find that "the kingdoms of this world are become the kingdoms of our Lord, and of his Christ; and he shall reign for ever and ever" (Rev. 11:15).

Before Christ becomes King of kings and Lord of lords He has already fulfilled God's promise that He would die on behalf of men. So He is the One who "loved us, and washed

us from our sins in his own blood" (Rev. 1:5). Christ first
must die to atone for our sins and reconcile us to God. Then
in His resurrection He gives us life, that He might live in us,
with the assurance of indestructible resurrection life at His
coming.

We who are saved are the recipients of God's great gifts.
These He has given to us without any strings attached. God
first showers His grace upon us and all His blessings follow,
for it is "grace unto us and peace." Peace does not belong to
us by nature but it follows from the grace of God working on
our behalf.

The love of God is an outgoing love, not a selfish one.
The outgoing love of God does something for us that He
wants to do for our benefit without our deserving it. It is
because of His love and grace that He has washed us from our
sins in the blood of Christ. We have been reconciled to God
and have been made free from sin's penalty and also from its
power if we will avail ourselves of what we have in Christ. No
such benefits belong to the unsaved.

A Kingdom and Priests

The passage goes on to say that Christ has "made us kings
and priests unto God and his Father; to him be glory and
dominion for ever and ever. Amen" (v. 6). The expression,
"made us kings and priests," is literally, "made us a kingdom,
priests unto God. . . ." Christ alone bears the title of King.

We who have trusted in Christ are joint heirs with Him
and are therefore subjects of His kingdom. We learn in
Colossians 1:13,14: "Who hath delivered us from the power
of darkness, and hath translated [transferred] us into the
kingdom of his dear Son: In whom we have redemption
through his blood, even the forgiveness of sins."

We also read in Revelation 20 that we shall reign with
Christ one thousand years. This means then that we are a
kingdom, that is, a body of redeemed, and our position is
indicated by the word "priests." A priest is a mediator or
go-between. Today the Lord is using us to represent Him to

the world. "Now then we are ambassadors for Christ, as though God did beseech you by us: we pray you in Christ's stead, be ye reconciled to God" (II Cor. 5:20).

In the last phrases of verse 6 of Revelation 1 the Apostle John ascribes glory and dominion to Christ forever and ever. Christ is the rightful heir to these. He had glory with the Father before the world began. Before He left the world in His earthly ministry He asked the Father that once again He might have the glory that was His previous to His Incarnation. God answered this in the affirmative. Christ's glory is that which comes with absolute righteousness which He always showed. Complete dominion is His also since He is King of kings and Lord of lords.

In the Book of the Revelation we see Christ presented some 28 times as a Lamb. This speaks about redemption. It is also stated that He is the Lamb worthy to take the kingdom which the Father will give Him. This kingdom is not given to Christ as the result of the faithful working of His saints on the earth who gradually bring that kingdom to pass. The program of the Church and of believers of the present day is to call out a people for Christ, not to bring in the kingdom for Him.

Psalm 110:1 says, "The Lord said unto my Lord, Sit thou at my right hand, until I make thine enemies thy footstool." This is something God does. Nowhere in the Scriptures are we taught that the millennial kingdom will be ushered in as the result of the work of men. We can enter the kingdom of God only through the new birth, for our Saviour said, "Except a man be born of water and of the Spirit, he cannot enter into the kingdom of God." Thus the spiritual phase of God's kingdom is entered only through the power of God. So also will that phase of the kingdom we call the millennial reign of Christ be established by divine power.

John then adds the word "Amen." This means "That is the truth and we agree with it, so let it be forever and ever."

Judgment and Restoration Announced

John declares in verse 7, "Behold, he cometh with clouds; and every eye shall see him, and they also which pierced him; and all kindreds of the earth shall wail because of him. Even so, Amen." The Second Coming of Christ is in two stages and the second stage is spoken of here. It is with the second stage of His Second Coming that Christ brings judgment, and following judgment, restoration of righteousness upon the earth.

The first stage of Christ's coming has to do with what we call the "Rapture." This is not a word found in the Bible. It means "a catching or snatching away" which is referred to in the original in I Thessalonians 4:13-18. Part of this reads: "For the Lord himself shall descend from heaven with a shout, with the voice of the archangel, and with the trump of God: and the dead in Christ shall rise first: Then we which are alive and remain shall be caught up together with them in the clouds, to meet the Lord in the air: and so shall we ever be with the Lord" (vv. 16,17). The expression "shall be caught up" is the translation of the word from which we get the idea of "rapture." It speaks of a sudden catching away; and in this context it has to do with the members of Christ's Body being caught up in the clouds to meet the Lord in the air.

This first stage of Christ's coming precedes the Tribulation which is described in the Book of the Revelation. Moreover, Christ does not come all the way to the earth at this first stage but simply into the clouds to meet us. In contrast to this, Revelation 1:7 speaks of Christ's coming with clouds to the earth, not just to the air.

In agreement with this is Acts 1:10,11: "And while they looked stedfastly toward heaven as he went up, behold, two men stood by them in white apparel; Which also said, Ye men of Galilee, why stand ye gazing up into heaven? this same Jesus, which is taken up from you into heaven, shall so come in like manner as ye have seen him go into heaven." The Lord Jesus was taken up from the earth and a cloud received Him

out of the sight of His disciples (Acts 1:9). Since He will
come in like manner, He will come back to the earth in the
clouds as promised.

The same truth is presented in Daniel 7:13,14 where it is
stated one like the Son of Man would come with the clouds
of heaven and would be given a kingdom on earth. This
coming to the earth follows the Tribulation. The Rapture of
the Church precedes the Tribulation.

Revelation 1:7 can very well serve as a key verse for the
study of the entire Book of the Revelation. The Book takes
up in detail events leading up to Christ's coming again to the
earth, telling of the things that will take place between His
coming into the air for His Church and the coming to the
earth to establish His kingdom.

"Behold, he cometh," says John. When is He coming?
This we have merely intimated as a coming following the
Tribulation and this is in line with Matthew 24:29,30:
"Immediately after the tribulation of those days shall the sun
be darkened, and the moon shall not give her light, and the
stars shall fall from heaven, and the powers of the heavens
shall be shaken: And then shall appear the sign of the Son of
man in heaven: and then shall all the tribes of the earth
mourn, and they shall see the Son of man coming in the
clouds of heaven with power and great glory." Nothing will
hold Him back when the time is ripe for Him to come.

Furthermore we are told in Revelation 1 that every eye
shall see Him. This is in contrast to the Rapture, the catching
away of the Church, which will more than likely be a secret
event rather than a public one. That, of course, will trigger
the time of the Tribulation, the last seven years of Daniel's
great prophecy. At the Revelation of Jesus Christ, that is,
when He comes to this earth after the Tribulation, every eye
shall see Him. Those who now think of Him with contempt
will see Him with their physical eyes and will be in terror at
the judgment facing them. He will right wrongs and will bring
into balance the things which are now out of balance in this
world. Many of God's people have been mistreated in this
world, but they are not to avenge themselves. They are to let

God even matters out. He will do this, though we may be raptured before any equalization is brought about by Him. We should lift up our heads, for our redemption draws near.

Believers of this age are not appointed unto the day of wrath but salvation. That means that the Christian of this age will not enter the time of Tribulation but enjoy the promise given in Revelation 3:10: "Because thou hast kept the word of my patience, I also will keep thee from the hour of temptation [testing], which shall come upon all the world, to try them that dwell upon the earth." We will not be on the earth during that time but will come with Him when He is seen coming in clouds. Those who have pierced Him and all the kindreds and tribes of the earth will wail because of Him when He comes as Judge.

At that time the rebellious world will see Him. They will have good reason to dread His appearance. We learn from Revelation 6:15, "And the kings of the earth, and the great men, and the rich men, and the chief captains, and the mighty men, and every bondman, and every free man, hid themselves in the dens and in the rocks of the mountains; And said to the mountains and rocks, Fall on us, and hide us from the face of him that sitteth on the throne, and from the wrath of the Lamb: for the great day of his wrath is come; and who shall be able to stand?" It is then that the nations of the earth shall mourn according to Matthew 24:30. Fear will be so great they will seek death. They will be utterly frustrated for they will not be able to find it.

John concludes verse 7 of Revelation 1 with the words: "Even so, Amen." This is not to be understood as John taking delight in the fact that the world will be judged when Jesus comes. It is rather his acknowledgement that such judgment is due. Jesus has been ill-treated ever since He came the first time. Men scorned Him then and crucified Him. Down through the years they have refused His love and spurned His offer of salvation. Such conditions cannot endure indefinitely. He must bring His offer of life to a close. He has waited nearly 2000 years now since His first coming, so the time of His vindication is near.

It is only a fool who will insist that a God of love would not do such a thing as described here in the Book of the Revelation. The offer of life has long been extended and His love continuously expressed. God's provision for escape from wrath has been offered to men down through the centuries, so it is now time for love to be vindicated. God is not only a God of love but also of righteousness. No God of righteousness could overlook man's constant and insistent rebellion. The offer to men now is as the Lord said in John 14:6: "I am the way, the truth, and the life: no man cometh unto the Father, but by me." The person who turns in faith to Christ now need not fear the wrath of God during the Tribulation, for the believers of this age will be in heaven with Christ probably at the Marriage Feast.

The last verse of the salutation is verse 8. Here the Lord Jesus says, "I am Alpha and Omega, the beginning and the ending, saith the Lord, which is, and which was, and which is to come, the Almighty."

Christ is both the Originator and the Consummator of all that exists. In Isaiah 44:6 we read, "I am the first, and I am the last; and beside me there is no God." Without Him there is no origin. And without Him there is no consummation of life. He is the sum total of it all.

Since He is the One who always was and who now is and always will be, He is the Jehovah of the Old Testament and the Christ of the New. He is the Almighty One. This is our consolation. Men have some might as the terrible power of the atom bomb shows. Satan is even mightier than man, for as Lucifer, the angel of light, he was the most powerful creature ever created by God. But Christ is Almighty. He will, according to His own pleasure, fulfill His purposes. Here is His great goal as stated in Ephesians 1:9,10: "Having made known unto us the mystery of his will, according to his good pleasure which he hath purposed in himself: That in the dispensation of the fulness of times he might gather together in one all things in Christ, both which are in heaven, and which are on earth; even in him."

We have noted that He is both the beginning and the end.

A series of comparisons between the first three chapters of Genesis and the first three chapters of the Book of the Revelation provide us with some glorious truths concerning Christ. Genesis, for example, is the Book of origin, whereas the Revelation is the Book of consummation. In Genesis we are brought face to face with a Triune God, the One who created the heavens and the earth. In Revelation 1:1-4 we are again brought face to face with the Triune God—Father, Son and Holy Spirit—who shall bring all things to a consummation.

In Genesis, chapter 1 we are introduced to material things as they were created by the Lord. In Revelation 1:7,8 Christ is referred to as the "Alpha and Omega"—emphasizing that He is not only the Originator of all things, but also the Consummator of all that is material.

In Genesis 1 and 2 we are introduced to the origin of all life, both physical and spiritual. But in Revelation 1:5,6 we see the cause of all spiritual life. That is due to Jesus Christ who is the first begotten from the dead and who has washed us in His own blood. We also see in Revelation the final destination of all spiritual life. It is in Revelation, the third chapter that we learn how spiritual life can begin for an individual. The Lord says, "Behold, I stand at the door and knock: if any man hear my voice, and open the door, I will come in to him, and will sup with him, and he with me." And then the words are added: "To him that overcometh will I grant to sit with me in my throne, even as I also overcame, and am set down with my Father in his throne." This last points us to the final destiny of those who are spiritually born again.

In Genesis 1:2 we read of God's presence hovering over an earth in darkness apparently judged because of sin that had come upon it (Satan's sin as seen in Isa. 14:12—17). Darkness, we are told, was upon the face of the deep. In Revelation 1:5 we find that Jesus Christ bore the judgment of sin upon Himself and so new life is given to all who dare believe in Him.

In Genesis 1:26 we see man created in God's image and

placed upon the earth to have dominion over it and all things on it. But man failed his original purpose because of sin. In contrast, in Revelation 1:6 we see the new man in Christ placed in a position to have all spiritual rule and spiritual dominion. He shall sit with Christ upon His throne.

In Genesis 3 we see the origin of man's sin. In Revelation 1:13-18 we see Christ as the great Priest King who will completely conquer sin.

In Genesis 3:15 and 21 we find the original promise of salvation made to men, and then the provision for the restoration of fallen man to fellowship with God. In Revelation 2 and 3 the letters to the churches reveal how men may continue this fellowship with God.

In Genesis 3:8,9 God makes it His personal affair to bring man back to Himself. He did not send an angel but came Himself. And so it is in Revelation 3:20. We find Christ personally standing at the door of our hearts, knocking and asking us to let Him in.

In Genesis 3 Satan came to demand worship and tried to persuade men to believe that God did not really love them. But in Revelation 3:9 we find that Satan and those with him will be brought to the redeemed and will worship at their feet, and God will prove that He loves His people.

In Genesis 3:24 we learn that God expelled man from Paradise, but in Revelation 2:7 the new Paradise is promised. Furthermore, in Revelation 3:21 a new position is assured for those who have overcome, for they shall sit with Christ in His throne.

Chapter Four

John's Vision of Christ
(Rev. 1:9-20)

An Apostle in Exile

In this next section of chapter 1, the Apostle John tells us where he was located when he received God's message, what he saw and what he was to do about it. Verses 9 and 10 read as follows: "I John, who also am your brother, and companion in tribulation, and in the kingdom and patience of Jesus Christ, was in the isle that is called Patmos, for the word of God, and for the testimony of Jesus Christ. I was in the Spirit on the Lord's day, and heard behind me a great voice, as of a trumpet."

John was getting along in years at this time, somewhere between 90 and 100 years of age, but his spiritual vision was undimmed. He was exiled on the Island of Patmos, a bleak, rocky island used by Rome for confining certain types of prisoners. The Apostle was completely separated from his friends and country because of his faithfulness in proclaiming the Word of God. To be thus shut away on a forsaken island 50 miles from the nearest city or town where any of his Christian friends might be located would be reason for despair for the ordinary person, but John was not ordinary.

There are times when all of us pass through experiences when we wonder if God has not forsaken us. We even question God's wisdom in allowing some trials to come into our lives. In reality He never forsakes us. Whatever He allows to come to us He works together for our good. John knew this and did not despair.

In reality he lived in two environments. He was on a desolate island with perhaps a few other prisoners, but at the same time he had the companionship of the Holy Spirit. And though it is within the power of men to separate Christians from each other and from other human beings, no man can shut out the Spirit of God from a believer or limit the testimony of Jesus Christ. Though John was physically confined to Patmos, God's testimony through him was not stifled.

Some of Paul's greatest epistles came from his pen while he was prisoner in Rome. The Epistle of Joy, the Letter to the Philippians, was included in that group. A Roman dungeon became the place from which God sent some of His richest truths to His people. Like John, Paul lived in two environments.

Many years later, John Bunyan was put in jail in Bedford, England, because he dared to preach the gospel. From that prison came *Pilgrim's Progress*, which has probably been translated into more languages than any other book except the Bible.

The Apostle John was shut away from his friends, but in the providence of God he was spiritually hemmed in to Christ. The Romans thought they had quarantined the gospel by making John a prisoner on Patmos, but there John found his greatest liberty in the Holy Spirit. His local, physical situation was that of a prisoner, but his spiritual consciousness was that of the freedom of the Spirit. Not only is man's extremity God's opportunity, but it also is often in the plans of God for His people to pass through experiences as did John.

Rome's attempt to shut off the witness of Christ brought John into such a place of solitude and closeness to his Saviour that he became the Lord's voice for the revelation of Jesus Christ as the Alpha and the Omega, the Beginning and the End.

How do we react to our lonelinesses? We should let God

be God in them. We may feel shut out from friends and loved ones even though we are in our homes and with families. God has put us in that situation for a special purpose. Let us go on with Him in it.

John said he was in the Spirit on the Lord's day. His experience was that of being carried beyond the normal senses into a state where God could reveal in a supernatural way the contents of the Book we now study. Apparently solitude was what John needed for these visions and solitude was what God provided.

It was in the Spirit that John was loosed from the normal boundaries of the flesh. He was transported into the future as God sees it. John was transported or projected beyond the time in which he lived. He was taken across the centuries to the time the Bible calls the Day of the Lord. That Day is the day of the consummation of all things material and spiritual. This will become very clear as these studies progress.

The writer to the Hebrews wrote: "See that ye refuse not him that speaketh. For if they escaped not who refused him that spake on earth, much more shall not we escape, if we turn away from him that speaketh from heaven: Whose voice then shook the earth: but now he hath promised, saying, Yet once more I shake not the earth only, but also heaven." Then follows the reason for this great final shaking, which in a large measure is the subject of the Book of the Revelation. "And this word, Yet once more, signifieth the removing of those things that are shaken, as of things that are made, that those things which cannot be shaken may remain." The great shaking is made so that the temporary things are removed. The permanent things will of course remain. The passage closes with the exhortation: "Wherefore we receiving a kingdom which cannot be moved, let us have grace, whereby we may serve God acceptably with reverence and godly fear: For our God is a consuming fire" (Heb. 12:25-29).

John's vision was largely concerning the future. What he saw had to do in a great measure with the end times. The expression "I was in the Spirit on the Lord's day" has been understood by many to mean Sunday or the first day of the week. This is how it is commonly used among us today. But in the Scriptures the Day of the Lord is an extended period of time in which Christ first deals in judgment on the earth and then sovereignly rules over it. It is used to cover the time of the Tribulation on through the Kingdom Age with the consummation of all things in the new heaven and the new earth. John was taken in the Spirit over the centuries to view the Day of the Lord as seen from both heaven's viewpoint and earth's viewpoint. It is described as God sees it and then also as men will see it upon the earth in that day.

John heard behind him a great voice as of a trumpet saying, "I am Alpha and Omega, the first and the last: and, What thou seest, write in a book, and send it unto the seven churches which are in Asia" (vv. 10,11). The seven specific churches the Lord had in mind are then named in the rest of the verse.

A very logical question that might have arisen in John's mind since he was a prisoner was how he could get his written message to the churches. John, however, was an obedient servant. Though the odds were against him, humanly speaking, he did not for a moment hedge on the commission God had given him. He wrote the message, knowing that God would see to it that it reached His people.

Some of us cannot even get the message across the neighbor's fence. Yet we are to be witnesses at home and abroad. John was in exile and he got the message out. He did his work with confidence because he knew the God who commissioned him.

The seven churches dealt with in this Book were not chosen at random. They are representative in several ways. They illustrate what can take place in any church in any time period; and they also clearly present the spiritual antidote for any wrong conditions. The information given describes accurately the local historical conditions in each of them in John's day. The admonitions and warnings given also serve as guidelines for local churches down through the years. There is also a prophetic element to these seven churches which provides a picture of the whole Church Age from John's day until the Rapture. Then, too, one must not overlook the personal message for the believer in these many admonitions and encouragements given to the overcomer.

In verses 12 and 13 we read: "And I turned to see the voice that spake with me. And being turned, I saw seven golden candlesticks; And in the midst of the seven candlesticks one like unto the Son of man, clothed with a garment down to the foot." The seven golden candlesticks were actually "golden lampstands." There is a difference between a candlestick which is self-consuming, and a lampstand which supports a lamp with a wick which is fed by oil and with proper care could burn continuously. According to verse 20 of this same chapter the lampstands represent the churches; so Christ is represented here as being in the midst of the churches. Christ is the light and the Holy Spirit is often referred to symbolically as oil. Thus it is through the Holy Spirit that the light of Jesus Christ is produced in us.

The Church itself is not the light; it is the light holder. Sometimes emphasis is put on the local church as though it were the light independent of anything else. God works through the local church, but it is not the church that shines but the light of Jesus Christ Himself shining through His people. Each individual church is to be a center of light.

Cooperative efforts among churches can be a blessing but they can also be a curse. If mere churchianity is aimed at, merely organization, then the light that the church is supposed to let shine is shut out. The ecumenical movement of the present day carries some real dangers in this respect. A church is a lightbearer only to the extent that it presents Christ as the Light shining in a dark world. The judgments warned of later on in the Revelation are tied in with failure to let this light shine.

Christ in the Midst

John was given to see a truth that we need to grasp today. Christ is in the midst of the churches and knows all that is going on. We do not see Him physically present; but even where two or three are gathered together in His name He is among them. Christ indwells each believer and also moves in the midst of His people.

In his Patmos vision John saw persons and things in heaven and on earth. And these persons and things were all vitally connected whether they were in heaven or on earth.

This is a phase of life we may not completely understand, but we have many illustrations of it in the Scriptures. In one of His last conversations with His disciples our Lord said, "Let not your heart be troubled: ye believe in God, believe also in me. In my Father's house are many mansions: if it were not so, I would have told you. I go to prepare a place for you. And if I go and prepare a place for you, I will come again, and receive you unto myself; that where I am there ye may be also. And whither I go ye know, and the way ye know. Thomas saith unto him, Lord, we know not whither thou goest; and how can we know the way? Jesus saith unto him, I am the way, the truth, and the life: no man cometh unto the Father, but by me" (John 14:1-6). So there are very vital links between heaven and earth. Christ who is the way to heaven is also the One who is in the midst of His churches on earth. As God He is present everywhere at the same time and is preparing His people on earth for their place in heaven. So, heaven is a prepared place for a prepared people, as someone has said.

For any of us to be ready or be prepared for heaven we must first be washed from our sins. This is the message of Revelation 1:5 where we read that Christ "washed us from our sins in his own blood." In Titus 3:5 Paul wrote: "Not by works of righteousness which we have done, but according to his mercy he saved us, by the washing of regeneration, and renewing of the Holy Ghost." In another place we are told that we must be born again or born from above (John 3:5). John wrote in his First Epistle: "He that hath the Son hath life; and he that hath not the Son of God hath not life" (5:12). Thus, in order to be prepared for heaven we must have the life the Lord Jesus gives. He Himself becomes our life.

Moreover, the person who is prepared for heaven is a person who will eventually be like Christ. We read in I John 3:2: "Beloved, now are we the sons of God, and it doth not yet appear what we shall be: but we know that, when he shall appear, we shall be like him; for we shall see him as he is."

Christ Has the Final Word

Christ has the final word as to our fitness to enter into His presence. In Revelation 1:17 John tells us: "And when I saw him, I fell at his feet as dead. And he laid his right hand upon me, saying unto me, Fear not; I am the first and the last: I am he that liveth, and was dead; and, behold, I am alive for evermore, Amen; and have the keys of hell and of death." He has passed through death for us but now He is alive and is therefore our life. He holds the key concerning those who will get into His presence in heaven.

Christ must and always will protect the holiness of God. Christ will not allow anyone to approach the Father's throne who is not as holy as He Himself is. This for us means that Christ becomes our holiness, for God sees us in Him. We need to be a prepared people if we are to get into heaven at all.

The Lord Jesus does not try to keep us out of heaven. We learn in this first chapter in Revelation that before He begins to pronounce judgment upon the world, He declares what He has provided for us so that we might escape judgment. The judgment we escape is not only such as will fall upon the earth in the Tribulation but also the judgment of the Great White Throne. This is eternal judgment or the second death.

Christ Described

The Lord Jesus Christ is described by John as clothed with a garment down to the foot, "and girt about the paps with a golden girdle. His head and his hairs were white like wool, as white as snow; and his eyes were as a flame of fire; And his feet like unto fine brass, as if they burned in a furnace; and his voice as the sound of many waters" (vv. 13-15).

The robe and the girdle reveal Christ to be in the place of final authority. There is none to dispute His rule. In Ephesians 1:20,21 we read of the power of God in Christ. "Which he wrought in Christ, when he raised him from the dead, and set him at his own right hand in the heavenly places, Far above all principality, and power, and might, and dominion, and every name that is named, not only in this world, but also in that which is to come."

This garment and girdle belong to Christ as a Priestly Judge. He is not only a Priest but He is also a Judge. We think of a judge as being stern and meting out sentences against evildoers. But the priest is one who speaks on behalf of the individual before another. So Christ is the Priestly Judge. The picture here is in keeping with the Old Testament description of a person filling both functions. Christ is presented in Revelation 1 as a Priestly Judge dealing in a compassionate way. Before He reveals what will take place against the enemies of God, He first comes to examine His own people.

Peter saw the right sequence of judgment when he wrote: "For the time is come that judgment must begin at the house of God: and if it first begin at us, what shall the end be of them that obey not the gospel of God? And if the righteous scarcely be saved, where shall the ungodly and the sinner appear?" (I Pet. 4:17,18). The Apostle is not telling us in this passage that it is going to be hard for any of us to be saved. What he says is that we in ourselves could never be saved. Salvation is a divine act on the part of God. He has made it possible through sending His Son into the world for us to have our sins forgiven and be assured of a place in heaven.

Then Peter goes on to point out that if this is all necessary in order to save those who are saved, what chance will the ungodly have in God's presence? It is impossible for them to stand. Christ is the Priestly Judge who as High Priest died for us, then as Judge He will keep those out of heaven who have refused to accept His life.

Since Christ, then, is the way to heaven and is completely

in control as to who will be admitted, the only safe place for anyone to be is in Christ. This is confirmed by Romans 8:1 which says, "There is therefore now no condemnation to them which are in Christ Jesus." Those who recognize that Christ is the way, the truth and the life and come unto the Father by Him are fully accepted by God.

Christ has the keys of hell and death; therefore, He has the right to say who goes where. We can rest assured that since He has come all the way from heaven to die for us as a sacrifice in our place, He will not refuse us heaven when we accept Him as Saviour. He wants to see us have the right to enter the heavenly glory. But those who continually refuse God's way into His presence will be shut out from heaven by the very One who could have led them in to heaven. Christ has the keys of hell and of death, and will open hell for those who are absolutely determined to reject His matchless love.

There is a tremendous contrast between the picture of the natural man in Romans 3 and the glorified Christ in Revelation 1. Concerning the natural man Paul writes: "There is none righteous, no, not one. There is none that understandeth, there is none that seeketh after God. They are all gone out of the way, they are together become unprofitable; there is none that doeth good, no, not one" (vv. 10-12). Christ, on the other hand, is presented to us in Revelation 1 as characterized by eternal purity. This is seen in the fact that His head and His hair are described as being white as wool, as white as snow. He is eternally pure and only that which is pure is eternal. So it is only when we are purified by Him that we have eternal life. His purity is the basis of His eternality, and His eternality is the crowning of His purity. He was pure eternally and He will live on in purity for eternity.

The natural man, however, is under sin. There is no purity in any of us in our natural state. There is every reason for us to turn to Him for salvation now. If we do not, then in the future we will have to meet Him in all His purity as Judge.

Eyes As Fire

John describes Christ as having "eyes . . . as a flame of fire" (v. 14). This speaks to us of infinite and infallible knowledge. The eyes of our Lord pierce and penetrate into every area and corner so that no secret can be kept from Him. He sees all things. He sees that which is evil and that which is good. Since He Himself is absolutely pure, He shuns evil and abhors it.

What Christ sees is seen accurately and truthfully. Thus He can arrive at a verdict that cannot be gainsaid. His knowledge of any subject is complete and His decision on it is final.

All men will eventually have to stand before Him. Even we who are Christians will have our works examined by Him. Paul wrote to the Corinthians: "For other foundation can no man lay than that is laid, which is Jesus Christ. Now if any man build upon this foundation gold, silver, precious stones, wood, hay, stubble; Every man's work shall be made manifest: for the day shall declare it, because it shall be revealed by fire; and the fire shall try every man's work of what sort it is. If any man's work abide which he hath built thereupon, he shall receive a reward. If any man's work shall be burned, he shall suffer loss: but he himself shall be saved; yet so as by fire" (I Cor. 3:11-15). Our Lord knows all about us and will carefully examine our conduct and ministry in order to reward us wherever He can. This indeed is wonderful.

There is no need of pretending before Him. We might deceive men but we cannot deceive Him. Ananias and Sapphira tried it according to the fifth chapter of Acts but they failed. God gave Peter special insight and discernment so that he saw through their lying.

The ability of our Lord to see all things is emphasized for us in Hebrews 4:13: "Neither is there any creature that is not manifest in his sight: but all things are naked and opened unto the eyes of him with whom we have to do." Jeremiah testified of this same truth when he recorded what the Lord said, "I the Lord search the heart, I try the reins [God tests the purposes in our lives], even to give every man according to his ways, and according to the fruit of his doings" (17:10). Does this inspire fear in your heart? Or is this an encouragement to you? This will depend on whether you are a child of God or not. A child of God will be inspired and encouraged by this revelation of God's power. One who is outside of God's family will be filled with fear. Then again a child of God who is not living as he should might have cause to fear the Judgment Seat of Christ.

David knew about this ability of God to see and know all things. He wrote about it in Psalm 139. This is a Psalm which we should read and reread time and again. And as we let God speak to our hearts through it, it will bring us joy and not fear. As long as there are sinful things, especially unconfessed sin, in our lives it will produce fear in us. But when we walk with God, confessing our failings to Him and getting daily cleansing from Him, then we will know what real joy is. God knows our sorrows and our works, whether good or bad, and every detail about us. The Psalmist ends the great Psalm with these words: "Search me, O God, and know my heart: try me, and know my thoughts: And see if there be any wicked way in me, and lead me in the way everlasting."

Man, on the other hand, in his natural state is in contrast to God in this respect. Romans 3:11,12 states: "There is none that understandeth, there is none that seeketh after God. They are all gone out of the way, they are together become unprofitable; there is none that doeth good, no, not one." From Adam's time on this has been true. Men don't search for God, He has to search for them. Man's natural way is to try to hide from God instead of seeking Him out. The natural man sees only a day at a time and that only in part. Man in his unsaved state has gone out of the way and has become unprofitable to God. The life of the natural man is a wasted life.

Feet As Fine Brass

In Revelation 1:15 it is said concerning Christ that "his feet [were] like unto fine brass, as if they burned in a furnace." Brass speaks of strength, and the furnace where brass has been burned speaks of purification. Brass also speaks of judgment, and in this case it would be pure judgment. All judgment has been committed by the Father into the hands of the Son so that the great Redeemer also becomes the mighty Judge.

Satan, of course, will be brought to judgment. The first statement concerning this appears in Genesis 3:15 where the Lord said to the serpent, "And I will put enmity between thee and the woman, and between thy seed and her seed [Satan's seed is the Antichrist and the woman's seed is Christ]; it shall bruise thy head [the seed of the woman would bruise Satan's head], and thou shalt bruise his heel [this was done when Jesus was crucified]." Nothing that is impure will last indefinitely. It will be judged. All sinful things will be brought to an end.

Our Lord also judges sin among His own people. We see Him pictured here as moving among the churches; but He always remains pure and never becomes contaminated with any of the evil He finds among them. There is no kind of power in the universe that can oppose Him in such a way as to stop either the fulfilling of His will or bring about the destruction of His work.

The Lord does not align Himself with anything in our lives that is not absolutely holy. The same is true with regard to our churches or our country. God will hold in derision the nations such as Russia that presently defy Him. This is true of any nation that forgets God. It could include our own where spiritual defection and moral blight are so evident.

In contrast to this is a portion in Romans 3 which tells us that the feet of men, that is natural men, "are swift to shed blood: Destruction and misery are in their ways" (vv. 15,16). Wherever men go they wreak havoc and ruin. Even for the sake of self-preservation man feels he must destroy others.

This shows, of course, man's inherent weakness. This is part of the reason for wars and rumors of wars among the nations. By nature man is contaminated with all kinds of evil. Beginning with Cain and on through until the present day man has killed to try and preserve the way of life he wanted. This was the reason Cain killed Abel.

The natural man in these United States of America is no different than the natural man anywhere else. We desire freedom, so we kill. But what freedoms do we really desire? Is it for our way of life which is not necessarily God's way of life?

His Voice

The voice of our Saviour is described as "the sound of many waters" (v. 15). When He speaks no other voices can be heard. He has brought a mighty message to this earth as we read in Hebrews 1:1-3: "God, who at sundry times and in divers manners spake in time past unto the fathers by the prophets, Hath in these last days spoken unto us by his Son, whom he hath appointed heir of all things, by whom also he made the worlds; Who being the brightness of his glory, and the express image of his person, and upholding all things by the word of his power, when he had by himself purged our sins, sat down on the right hand of the Majesty on high."

While there may be many messengers of the gospel, there is only one real Voice or one Word. That is the word of power in redemption or in intercession or even a warning of judgment to come. In any case it is the voice of love. God in His compassion for lost men tries to get the message of His grace through to them by using whomever He can.

When the Lord Jesus comes for His own, it will be with the shout, a voice of compassion and of love "for the Lord himself shall descend from heaven with a shout, with the voice of the archangel, and with the trump of God: and the dead in Christ shall rise first" (I Thess. 4:16). Our Lord prefers to deal with man in grace; and He always speaks in love before He is forced by man's rebellion and hostility to warn of judgment.

But what about man, the natural man? Romans 3 tells us: "Their throat is an open sepulchre; with their tongues they have used deceit; the poison of asps is under their lips: Whose mouth is full of cursing and bitterness" (vv. 13,14). What a terrible description of the mouth of the natural man. His is a voice that speaks curses and expresses bitterness. His throat is like a gaping tomb, speaking words of death, not life.

We also read concerning Christ that "he had in his right hand seven stars" (v. 16). The seven stars are the messengers of the seven churches. Being in His right hand they are in the place of perfect rest, perfect power and perfect protection. Is that where we find our rest? If not, the invitation is open to us. The Psalmist says, "Hold up my goings in thy paths, that my footsteps slip not. Shew thy marvellous lovingkindness, O thou that savest by thy right hand them which put their trust in thee from those that rise up against them. Keep me as the apple of the eye, hide me under the shadow of thy wings" (Ps. 17:5,7,8).

The Sharp Sword

The description of Christ continues in verse 16. There we learn: "And out of his mouth went a sharp twoedged sword: and his countenance was as the sun shineth in his strength." It is obvious that the sword described in this passage is not a literal, metal sword but the Word of God itself. The key to this is Hebrews 4:12: "For the word of God is quick [alive and active], and powerful, and sharper than any twoedged sword, piercing even to the dividing asunder of soul and spirit . . . and is a discerner of the thoughts and intents of the heart."

Christ speaks the word and condemns the false and approves the true. His word is a word of judgment in the sense of the Judgment Seat of Christ where He will evaluate the believer's works. He speaks words of judgment also with regard to the unsaved. We read in Revelation 19:15: "And out of his mouth goeth a sharp sword [the Word], that with it he should smite the nations: and he shall rule them with a rod of iron."

The power of the Word of God spoken by the Son of God is something to be reckoned with. Isaiah wrote: "And he shall smite the earth with the rod of his mouth, and with the breath of his lips shall he slay the wicked" (Isa. 11:4).

With regard to the Antichrist the Word of God says, "And then shall that Wicked be revealed, whom the Lord shall consume with the spirit of his mouth, and shall destroy with the brightness of his coming" (II Thess. 2:8). Men will not be able to escape Christ's spoken word at any time, for we read in John 12:48: "He that rejecteth me, and receiveth not my words, hath one that judgeth him: the word that I have spoken, the same shall judge him in the last day." There is no excuse, at least for persons in North America and in many other areas of the world. The Bible is still the most sold Book in the world today. It is true that many people may not have a copy, but it is quoted on radio, it is published in book form, and it is, at least in portions, given in periodicals. The Bible, either in part or whole, is available to large areas in the world today.

What a contrast is drawn in the Word between Christ whose lips speak the Word of God and the natural man whose mouth is filled with other things. The Bible says about the natural man: "Their throat is an open sepulchre: with their tongues they have used deceit; the poison of asps is under their lips: Whose mouth is full of cursing and bitterness. There is no fear of God before their eyes" (Rom. 3:13,14,18). This is the natural man as God sees him. This may not be our evaluation of the natural man because being men ourselves we tend to look on the outward appearance, whereas God looks on the heart (I Sam. 16:7). The only difference between men who are unsaved with regard to the description just given is that of degree but not of kind.

Though it is true of the natural man that there is no fear of God before his eyes, a time will come when all men will have to meet Christ face to face. Those who have rejected will fear Him then.

The Psalmist described man in these words: "The transgression of the wicked saith within my heart, that there is no fear of God before his eyes. For he flattereth himself in his own eyes, until his iniquity be found to be hateful. The words of his mouth are iniquity and deceit: he hath left off to be wise, and to do good" (Ps. 36:1-3). Man is so proud and self-confident that no matter what he does he thinks he will get by. Communism says, "There is no God." But this statement does not change the facts. Men know there is a God, and the only reason they deny He exists is because "the poison of asps is under their lips." Such men live in open defiance of God.

Have we as believers in Christ recognized God in all His holiness? We will have to account for every idle word at the Judgment Seat of Christ. There will be no condemnation of believers there, for there is "no condemnation to them which are in Christ Jesus" (Rom. 8:1). But there will be careful scrutiny and evaluation of what we did and said as believers. Surely we want to have the best record possible before God.

I once heard a man say that he would rather go through the horrors of the Great Tribulation than to stand at the Judgment Seat of Christ having to answer for some things that some professing Christians have done. We dare not take either time or eternity lightly.

His Countenance

The Lord Jesus is also described as having His countenance "as the sun shining in his strength" (v. 16). What could stand in the blaze of the glory of the Son of God? He has absolute and final authority. Concerning Him Jeremiah wrote: "But the Lord is the true God, he is the living God, and an everlasting king: at his wrath the earth shall tremble, and the nations shall not be able to abide his indignation" (Jer. 10:10).

An awesome picture of Jesus Christ is given in Revelation 20. The Apostle wrote, "And I saw a great white throne, and him that sat on it [this is Jesus Christ], from whose face the earth and the heaven fled away; and there was found no place for them" (v. 11). The blasphemy and boasting of unregenerate men will be silenced in that day. No man can stand in the glory of Christ's presence.

As we have already seen, even the Antichrist will be defeated by the very presence of Christ. "And then shall that Wicked be revealed, whom the Lord shall consume with the spirit of his mouth, and shall destroy with the brightness of his coming" (II Thess. 2:8).

This is in direct contrast to Christ's first coming to the earth. We have this description of Him in Isaiah 52:14: "As many were astonied at thee; his visage was so marred more than any man, and his form more than the sons of men." The prophet continued in 53:2: "For he shall grow up before him as a tender plant, and as a root out of a dry ground: he hath no form nor comeliness; and when we shall see him, there is no beauty that we should desire him." This was Christ in His humanity and His humility. But today He is in the heavens, and when He returns to the earth again His countenance will be as the sun shining in its strength.

Man's only hope lies in Christ. He is the One who was dead but is alive and gives life to all who trust Him. This is eternal life that will never end. Nothing can separate His loved ones from Him. God cannot overlook sin, but God wants to help the sinner. How can God be the Justifier of ungodly men? Only because Christ has taken the sinner's place and through His substitutionary death has loosed us from our sins. In His perfect love He has offered us His righteousness which comes through faith in Him (Rom. 3:21,22).

It is no wonder that when John received his vision of the Lord Jesus Christ, he fell at His feet as though he were dead. No man can see Him and live except one who is in possession of Christ's life.

We as human beings in our present form are readily overcome by any display of the supernatural. A good illustration of this is found in Matthew 28:2-4: "And, behold, there was a great earthquake: for the angel of the

Lord descended from heaven, and came and rolled back the stone from the door, and sat upon it. His countenance was like lightning, and his raiment white as snow: And for fear of him the keepers did shake, and became as dead men." This was the reaction of unbelieving men to the presence of an angel. Angels are created beings just as men are created beings, but even the presence of an angel of God was sufficient to engender fear in those rough soldiers.

When Saul, who later became the Apostle Paul, met Christ on the road to Damascus, he was overcome and was blind for several days as a result of the glory of the Person who met him.

When the inner glory of Christ showed through the outer shell of His humanity on the Mount of Transfiguration, the Disciples were overcome. John the Apostle, though he had long been in the service of his Lord and had been one of the inner circle during Christ's ministry, could not stand before the glory of Christ's appearance.

Yet the appearance of Christ in this fashion to His own people is not for the purpose of terrifying them but to console them. The Lord Jesus laid His hand on John and said, "Fear not; I am the first and the last." The very majesty and sovereignty of God is a terror to the wicked but a comfort to the born-again saint. There is no need for those who trust Him to fear Him, for He is the Author of their life and also its Sustainer.

Christ is the Eternal One; man's eternity comes from Him. Even those who do not believe have eternal existence. Those who trust Him have eternal life. There is no annihilation, not even of angels. What is your relationship to this Christ of the Bible?

Our life in Christ is guaranteed as Peter writes: "Who are kept by the power of God through faith unto salvation ready to be revealed in the last time" (I Pet. 1:5). Or as Paul states it in Ephesians 1:13,14: "In whom ye also trusted, after that ye heard the word of truth, the gospel of your salvation: in whom also after that ye believed, ye were sealed with that holy Spirit of promise, Which is the earnest of our inheritance until the redemption of the purchased possession, unto the praise of his glory." In writing to Timothy, Paul gave the same assurance saying, "I know whom I have believed, and am persuaded that he is able to keep that which I have committed unto him against that day" (II Tim. 1:12).

Christ is the Eternal Christ and is the first and the last. He is the Christian's eternal life. We owe our eternity to Him. As we have already stated, even those who do not believe will exist eternally and those who trust Him will live forever. The unending life of angels also depends on Him who is the Living One.

Nevertheless, this One who is eternal entered into death. He came to this earth for the period of 33 years and at the end of that time He gave up His life on behalf of sinful men. But He did not remain in the grave. He arose triumphant over death. He is alive and has the keys of death and hell.

The reference to "keys" in this context means that Christ is sovereign in the area of physical death. Such death terminates man's life on this globe, yet no one dies without God's permission. Our lives are in His hands. Even though God permitted Satan to test Job, He did not allow the Evil One to take Job's life. During the Tribulation, according to Revelation 9, one of the great judgments loosed upon the earth will involve the torment of men for five months by evil spirits. Nevertheless, though men will seek death at that time, they will not find it. The Scripture says, "And in those days shall men seek death, and shall not find it; and shall desire to die, and death shall flee from them." The key to death lies in the hands of Christ.

Our Lord wrested the authority and power of death from Satan when He took upon Himself flesh and blood "that through death he might destroy him that had power of death, that is, the devil; And deliver them who through fear of death were all their lifetime subject to bondage" (Heb. 2:14,15). Death is not the chance thing that many consider it to be.

Christ also has the keys of hell or more correctly, *hades*. That is the place of the spirits of the unbelieving dead. Before Christ's resurrection it also contained a Paradise section where the believing dead were in comfort and rest. Since His resurrection and ascension, Paradise has been removed to the third heaven, so that when believers die now they go immediately into the presence of the Lord. As Paul states the truth in II Corinthians 5:8, death to the Christian means to be absent from the body and present with the Lord.

The Divine Outline of Revelation

John was commanded to "write the things which thou has seen, and the things which are, and the things which shall be hereafter" (Rev. 1:19). This is a key verse in Revelation, for it provides the outline of the Book as furnished by the Holy Spirit.

A threefold division is given here. First of all, John was to write the things which he had seen. The vision of Christ in chapter 1 is covered in this section. John saw the living Christ as He is today in His eternal glory. John wrote this down as he was instructed.

The second division has to do with "the things which are." That had to do with the time in which John was living and the period covered by the Church Age. This information is given in chapters 2 and 3 and shows the relationship of the Living Christ with the Church throughout its history.

The third division had to do with the "things which shall be hereafter." These are the events following the Church Age. This section begins with chapter 4 of the Revelation on through to the end of the Book. It covers the subject of the Tribulation, the establishing of Christ's earthly kingdom and finally, the new heaven and the new earth. With this key to understanding the Book there need be no confusion with regard to the main elements in the Book, neither considering it all fulfilled in history nor spiritualizing it so as to rob it of its clear and literal elements.

We will find that when we come to them, the letters to the seven churches are a very significant part of the Book of the Revelation. Christ is pictured as in the midst of them, examining them, telling what is wrong about them and what is good about them. He warns and encourages. Consequently what is said about the churches is not hearsay but direct statements from the Lord Himself. We should not be surprised that He says He is in the midst of the churches for this is in line with what He promised just before His ascension, according to Matthew 28:18-20. The Lord commissioned His disciples to go to all nations, preaching the gospel, and He gave this promise: "Lo, I am with you alway, even unto the end of the world [age]."

In this glorious picture of Christ He is represented as being completely clothed down to the foot. This was the opposite of Adam who when he sinned found himself to be naked. Our Lord was stripped of His clothing when He died for us on Calvary, but now He has been appointed High priest and Judge and as such He is fully clothed with the authority of Deity upon Him.

He also has the girdle of authority which was given Him because in His coming to this earth He emptied Himself of His heavenly glory and took on the form of a servant. He was made in the likeness of man and was obedient unto death, even the death of the cross. Now God has highly exalted Him and given Him a name which is above every name. So it is as the One with absolute authority in the universe that He examines and warns and comforts the churches.

His examination of the churches is not confined to just congregations as such. The individual is very much included. The churches are made up of persons and each person is closely examined by the Saviour.

He moves in the midst of the churches as the Ancient of Days who sees all things; not as men see them but as God sees them. Nothing escapes His penetrating gaze.

He also stands among them as the rightful Judge. He was judged on the cross because of our sins, but now as the resurrected Christ all judgment has been committed into His hand. What He commands cannot be successfully defied. All will have to listen whether they want to or not. Even those in the graves will at the right time hear His voice and come forth. His word is final.

No high, earthly court can set aside what He says or misinterpret His meaning.

His face reflects the glory of God. His identity cannot be questioned. All men will know Him when they see Him. We learn from Revelation 6 that men of high and low stations in life will want to hide from His face. They will recognize Him as their Judge, but nothing they can do will provide escape for them.

Christ is the Creator and Redeemer. By His word all things came into being, and by His word all things will be consummated. This is the Christ revealed to us in the Book of the Revelation. Men in their foolishness and wickedness of heart are trying to tell us that this world came into being through the process of evolution. They don't want to acknowledge a Creator. But denying His creatorship will not effect their escape from His judgeship. Their imaginations won't substitute for the facts. He is Victor over death, for though He died He is now alive. Death could not hold Him. His power is the power of Deity and is out of all man's comprehension.

In spite of the remarkable scientific achievements of men in these days, they have not overcome death. All men die sometime or another with the exception of those who have trusted in Christ and will be transformed at His coming for His Church. In Christ's hands are the keys of death and *hades*. He is supreme.

Chapter Five

The Church in Ephesus
(Rev. 2:1-7)

Introduction to Seven Churches

In chapters 2 and 3 of Revelation we have the letters to seven representative churches. These, as we have noted previously, present God's truth to us from several different angles. First of all, we recognize that these churches existed in the first century of the Christian era and apparently were chosen by the Lord for what He could say concerning them that would be of lasting value for churches down through the years. They carry a spiritual message for churches at any time and also apply to individual believers as does all the Word of God. One other message, however, is very significant and this we will emphasize. These seven churches chosen out of the many in existence at that time present to us church history in seven different stages.

If I were to give a title to this section I would call it "The Great Apostasy of the Last Days Traced From the Beginning of the Church's History." We will see how Satan uses what I call "the whittling method" of cutting away the essential features that make a church a church and finally makes it an arm of apostasy.

Apostasy is defection from truth, revolt against it, and abandonment of what one has voluntarily professed, or a total departure or desertion from one's faith or renunciation of it. This is a very serious matter; it began early in church

67

history and will be consummated in the world after the true Church is gone. This decline in faith can be traced through these seven churches with the climax reached in the great apostate church of Revelation 17.

The study of apostasy indicates that those who became apostates were once on the inside of the church. This is not too hard to understand when we realize that salvation is not attained by joining something but is a matter of inner faith. It is easy enough for one who has no faith to join a visible organization. Thus a person can be in an organization of a religious nature and yet have no real faith in his heart.

Down through the years many have professed Christianity who have never really possessed Christ. This was true even in the Apostolic era when the Apostle John tells us that some "went out from us, but they were not of us." By studying the gradual decay of the church through the ages, we will see how generation after generation gradually increased in apostasy, producing an alarming situation which confronts the church of the present day.

Chapters 2 and 3 as seen from this standpoint were prophetic in John's day but are almost entirely history for us now.

It is no accident that seven churches were chosen as representative churches in this section. From the first chapter of Genesis on through the whole Bible God's work runs in cycles of sevens. In Genesis 1 we find how He created the earth and the heavens in six days and on the seventh day He rested. A seven-year cycle was very significant in Israel's history, throughout the Old Testament. When we come to the last book in the Bible, the Book of Consummation, the number seven occurs 54 times. So it is in keeping with this principle that God has chosen these seven churches to present us with a complete course of church history from Pentecost to the Rapture, the catching away of the Church to be with Christ.

Church History Portrayed

Each letter to a specific church describes dominant characteristics of a particular period of church history. We have the advantage of looking back over these things today and can readily see how these various periods correspond with what is presented in these letters.

The first letter, that to Ephesus, provides a good picture of the spiritually powerful apostolic church of the first century.

The letter to Smyrna covers the martyr period of the church, the second and third centuries during which various pagan Roman rulers persecuted God's people.

Pergamos pictures the corruption of Christian testimony through the uniting of the church and the state under Constantine. This laid the foundation for the strong influence of the church during the fourth and fifth centuries.

The letter to Thyatira deals with the period of the Dark Ages from the sixth century on through the fifteenth. Elements of that darkness still persist today, however, and will continue on to the climax of apostasy in the end times.

The letter to Sardis describes for us the rise and development and finally the corruption of Protestantism. The Reformation which was a powerful movement in its beginning did not maintain its strong spiritual emphasis indefinitely.

Many Bible students are convinced that the letters to the Church in Philadelphia and Laodicea picture church conditions running side by side preceding the Church's Rapture. Philadelphia illustrates that which is genuine and true to the Lord Jesus Christ. Laodicea illustrates that which is false. Thus, the conditions pictured by Philadelphia and Laodicea can be easily discerned in Christendom today in many denominations and communities and even local churches.

It is significant that each of the last four letters suggest Christ's Second Coming. The characteristics of these four churches do not end with the period they depict but continue until the Day of Jesus Christ. This shows us that the corrupt world church, spiritually dead Protestantism, apostate modernism and genuine Bible-believing Christianity will continue simultaneously side by side until the Church is raptured.

The first letter, written to Ephesus, shows that Christ is neglected in the very beginning of church history. That sin of neglect was never properly corrected and it deepens and increases until we find Christ, in the seventh letter, outside the church entirely. In Laodicea He is pictured outside dealing with individuals.

These studies are not to be construed as an attack upon the Church of our Lord Jesus Christ as such. The true Church constitutes the Body of Christ, and we have His assurance that the gates of hell shall not prevail against it. But to borrow words from David, "Is there not a cause?" when we look at Christendom today. The apostasy is upon us and Christ is dishonored in many, many places.

The Church in Ephesus

The very first words to Ephesus are, "Unto the angel of the church of Ephesus write; These things saith he that holdeth the seven stars in his right hand, who walketh in the midst of the seven golden candlesticks." In each of the letters to the churches a portion of Christ in His glory is emphasized. Here He is described as in the midst of the churches holding the servants of the churches in His hand. He is right where the action is taking place. He tells what He sees, both what is good and what is wrong, all of which is firsthand information, nothing of it hearsay.

Verse 2 reads, "I know thy works, and thy labour, and thy patience, and how thou canst not bear them which are evil: and thou hast tried them which say they are apostles, and are not, and hast found them liars: And hast borne, and hast patience, and for my name's sake hast laboured, and hast not fainted." Here we have another characteristic of our Lord's approach to these churches. He usually starts out commending them for what is good. And not until He has done that does He point out what is wrong. Nothing can escape His penetrating gaze. And what He sees He evaluates properly. We are prone to criticize when we see something wrong and overlook what is good. That is natural with us but not with Christ. He indwells the believer and because He is omniscient He knows all things.

The word "labour" is used in this passage. It is a very significant word meaning toil, and strenuous, exhausting effort. The Lord says to Ephesus, "You really put forth a lot of effort. You have exhausted yourself in doing My work." A phrase often heard is, "I would rather wear out than rust out." Apparently that is what is being spoken of here. The believers in Ephesus worked themselves into a state of exhaustion for the sake of Christ. Their labor cost them something. David carried this principle in his heart when he said at one time, "Neither will I offer burnt-offerings unto the Lord my God of that which doth cost me nothing" (II Sam. 24:24). The church at Ephesus was hard working.

The Lord also said to them, "I know thy patience." This is the kind of patience that endures and still retains a forward drive. These believers kept on going in the work of Christ. They were steadfast in their endurance, refusing to give up. This is indeed commendable.

The Lord continued to praise them by saying, "Thou canst not bear them which are evil." The tendency in these modern times is to try to be at peace with everything about us. This can make Christians carelessly neglectful of a true sense of righteousness. These Ephesians had a holy abhorrence of all that was morally and spiritually bad. They would have none of it.

In our day many think only of peace at any price. We find many Christians more interested in peace than in purity of doctrine. Yet the only basis on which the ecumenical structure of our day could grow to the glory of God is on pure doctrine. But when any person raises the issue of doctrine, the plea is made that the man of God should put peace ahead of truth. This, of course, will end in the great apostate church of the last days.

False Apostles

The Lord Jesus went on to say, "Thou hast tried them which say they are apostles, and are not, and hast found them liars." We are admonished in the Word to check all teachers for what they teach and how they live. The Apostle John in his First General Epistle tells us we are to reject those who deny that Jesus Christ is come in the flesh. Our church circles are plagued today by so-called Christian leaders who do not believe that Jesus Christ is eternal and who do not believe He is the virgin-born Son of God.

The apostles were very careful to lay a groundwork of true doctrine for the early Christians to follow. Paul said in one place, "And my speech and my preaching was not with enticing words of man's wisdom, but in demonstration of the Spirit and of power: That your faith should not stand in the wisdom of men, but in the power of God" (I Cor. 2:4,5). Then to the Ephesians Paul wrote: "That we henceforth be no more children, tossed to and fro, and carried about with every wind of doctrine, by the sleight of men, and cunning craftiness, whereby they lie in wait to deceive."

Some teachers are dangerous because they teach only part truth. They mix truth with error which confuses Christians who may not be too mature in their spiritual knowledge. Then there are the outright apostates who deny the deity of Jesus Christ, deny that He is Creator, deny His blood atonement, deny His virgin birth, and mock at the idea of His Second Coming.

The church in Ephesus examined all teachers who came to them and repudiated those who did not preach the truth. They did not hesitate to expose and expel false apostles.

It is true that we do not have apostles in our day in the technical sense of the word as it is used in the New Testament. At first there were the 12 Apostles, then others such as Barnabas, Paul, and James—a half brother of Jesus. Our Lord Himself was called "the Apostle and High Priest of our profession." An apostle was a messenger authorized to act or speak for him who sent him.

Then a true messenger or apostle from the Lord had power and authority in keeping with his commission. This is clear from one of the last actions our Saviour took part in before His ascension. He came to the Disciples and said, "Peace be unto you: as my Father hath sent me, even so send I you. And when he had said this, he breathed on them, and saith unto them, Receive ye the Holy Ghost" (John 20:21,22). This action clearly indicated that when the Holy Spirit came in answer to Christ's prayer, He would empower the messengers of the gospel for their ministry.

The power and influence of true apostles were such that certain evil men sought the position and pretended to have the power. Since the New Testament was not quite completed until John's last years, there were always teachers claiming to have a message inspired of God. All of these had to be tested by the churches.

Paul warned about false teachers in these words: "For such are false apostles, deceitful workers, transforming themselves into the apostles of Christ. And no marvel; for Satan himself is transformed into an angel of light. Therefore it is no great thing if his ministers also be transformed as the ministers of righteousness; whose end shall be according to their works" (II Cor. 11:13-15). The church at Ephesus knew this strategy of Satan to get his false teachers in among God's people, so they did not hesitate to put to the test men who claimed to be messengers of God.

We must also be alert in our day and not assume that all who claim to be God's messengers are, indeed, from Him. The test must go deeper than merely agreement or disagreement with our church creed or denominational teaching. Creeds can be wrong. A true test of teachers must be on the basis of what the Word of God teaches. It is the final authority on what is true and false.

In Ephesus these false apostles were tested and found to be liars. They were untruthful and deceitful.

Tests for Teachers

The Word of God gives us various tests by which to examine men and their teaching. Several are given in John's First General Epistle. In I John 1:8 we read: "If we say that we have no sin, we deceive ourselves, and the truth is not in us." Here is one, then, devoid of truth, self-deceived and apparently trying to influence others to the same wrong position.

In verse 10 of the same chapter the Apostle writes, "If we say that we have not sinned, we make him a liar, and his word is not in us." Words are not wasted here. Those who say they are not sinful enough to be lost are characterized as liars.

Another phase of deceit and untruth is uncovered in I John 2:22: "Who is a liar but he that denieth that Jesus is the Christ? He is antichrist, that denieth the Father and the Son." Anyone who says that Jesus Christ is not virgin-born, that He is not God, that He did not come to this earth in human form to be man's Redeemer, that person is a liar. He is a false teacher.

Some of these tests can come very close to how we live, for John points out in I John 4:20: "If a man say, I love God, and hateth his brother, he is a liar." Then in 5:10,11 he says, "He that believeth on the Son of God hath the witness in himself: he that believeth not God hath made him a liar; because he believeth not the record that God gave of his Son. And this is the record, that God hath given to us eternal life, and this life is in his Son." These are not complicated tests but they go to the very heart of the Christian faith. When teachers deny that Jesus Christ is the Eternal Son of God who came to die for our sins and try to pass Him off as a martyr for a great cause, we know from the Word that such men are false teachers. They are not messengers from God giving the truth of God, but are emissaries of Satan.

Leaving the First Love

After commending the church in Ephesus for its ministry and labors the Lord, who was in the midst of His people closely examining not only their conduct but also their very hearts, pointed out that they had left their first love.

I use the word "whittler" to describe one of Satan's most effective methods of destroying the effectiveness of our work for Christ. Outstanding biblical error and apostasy do not show up all at once among God's people. They are preceded by Satan's whittling process. One evil weakness yielded to or tolerated prepares for the next. The departure from God's established Word is made by degrees, not all at once. Satan gained his first foothold in the church of Ephesus by getting them to put their service for Christ ahead of their love for the Person of Christ. The Evil One could not get them to deny their faith nor to become indifferent toward the truth of the gospel. They loved that truth and tested men who came in their midst claiming to be from God. But Satan succeeded in striking them at the very heart of their spiritual lives and succeeded in forcing a wedge between them and their first love for the Saviour.

Christ said to Ephesus that there was some love for Him, but the first love was gone. He appreciated their labors and the fact that they had kept their house doctrinally clean. He commended them for their good works, but He could not in faithfulness to them overlook their neglect.

What about us? Do we merely labor or do we have time for fellowship with our Lord? I shall never forget something that took place in our family after my wife and I had been married for some six or seven years. We had two children by then, but since I was very busy in evangelism, frequently gone for one or two weeks at a time, I did not see much of my little family. It was hard on them. By God's grace and help I was taking care of my "bread and butter" responsibility to them, but since I was so occupied with the work I did not miss them as much as they missed me.

Then one day when I was home my wife put her arms

around me and said, "Honey, do you still love us? Or is it merely duty now for your family?"

As I stood there I awakened to something I had never thought of. It had not dawned on me that I could become so busy in my work for the Lord that I was neglecting my own loved ones. That awakening changed a lot of things with regard to our home life.

It is possible for us to labor for our Lord to the place where we have no time for fellowship with Him. And the charge He made to His people in Ephesus was not that they had lost their first love but that they had "left" it. We can sometimes lose something we don't want to lose; but to leave something could mean a deliberate choice to leave it. We might say that these early Christians had abandoned their first love because they had become so occupied with service.

What is this first love that is sometimes called the "foremost" love? It is complete devotion to Christ, not merely religious duty. It is heart devotion that has no thought for self.

It is the kind of love that Christ Himself had. Paul described this in writing to the Philippians: "Keep on fostering the same disposition that Christ Jesus had. Though He was existing in the nature of God, He did not think His being on an equality with God a thing to be selfishly grasped, but He laid it aside as He took on the nature of a slave and became like other men. Because He was recognized as a man, in reality as well as in outward form, He finally humiliated Himself in obedience so as to die, even to die on a cross" (Phil. 2:5-8, *Williams*).

This is a self-denying love that abandons all for Christ. We love Him supremely who did so much for us. This is a love that defies analysis but it can be expressed through us because it has been shed abroad in our hearts by the Holy Spirit (Rom. 5:5). It goes far beyond filial love for which men have a natural capacity. It is not merely human friendship or looking with personal heart emotion. In fact, it is not emotion at all, but something that springs from a sense of value placed on that which one loves.

These early Christians had become occupied with past accomplishments, present works and future plans more than with Christ Himself. Christian activity had displaced spiritual fellowship.

Evidences of Lack of Love

It is easy to become like Martha who became so occupied working for Christ that she missed being like Him. Her work became a burden and she asked the Lord to tell Mary, her sister, to help her. Mary had been listening to what the Saviour had to say. Jesus answered, "Martha, thou art careful and troubled about many things: But one thing is needful: and Mary hath chosen that good part, which shall not be taken away from her" (Luke 10:41,42).

Spiritual pride often arises and when it does it replaces pure spiritual life. This is the result of activity, Christian activity, with neglect of spiritual fellowship with the Lord. When we fail to take time to be alone with Him, our service can easily become a matter of pride to us. No genuine servant of God ever departed from the faith without first departing from his private devotional life with Christ.

How much time do we spend with Him in the morning? Fifteen minutes? Is that the measure of our love for Him? We must ever remember that Christian activity alone robs us of our personal fellowship with Christ, robs us of spiritual usefulness. If we really love Christ we will keep His commandments. It will not be a matter of we "ought" to keep His commandments but we "will" keep them. Fellowship with Him produces the right kind of spiritual activity.

We often evidence our lack of love by listening to men instead of to what God says. We don't take time for His Word. If we get under conviction from what God says, there is an urgency that lays hold of us. But if it is merely a man speaking to us, we can shake that off very easily.

Paul said that Christ's love compelled him to listen and labor. Samuel said, "Speak; for thy servant heareth." Our spiritual progress lies not merely in what we do but in what we are, for the doing will come from the being.

We have good reason to deplore some of the things found in the organized church today. The apostasy, the ecumenical movement, the spiritual lethargy are all threats to the church's future. Yet these things all started 1900 years ago in a situation in the church at Ephesus which was never corrected.

The same danger threatens a number of our fundamental evangelical churches of the present day. They would not harbor anything that is not orthodox—not in line with Scripture—but their witness is poor and they see few souls saved. The trouble is they have left their first love. Like Ephesus they did not lose it but either deliberately abandoned it or became so concerned with activity that they neglected it. And as with the church, so it is with an individual Christian; spiritual effectiveness comes from what we are in our relationship to Christ. Deeds and activity that count come from a quality of life that is in fellowship with Christ.

Paul prayed a remarkable prayer for the Ephesians, this very church that Jesus charged with having left their first love. The Apostle prayed: "That he [Christ] would grant you, according to the riches of his glory, to be strengthened with might by his Spirit in the inner man" (Eph. 3:16). Paul continued, "That Christ may dwell in your hearts by faith; that ye, being rooted and grounded in love, May be able to comprehend with all saints what is the breadth, and length, and depth, and height; And to know the love of Christ, which passeth knowledge, that ye might be filled with all the fulness of God" (vv. 17-19).

How does something become spiritually rooted and grounded? It has to do with our devotional life concerning the Person of Jesus Christ. Is your time with Him in the morning a precious time? Or do you quickly read Scripture and let it go at that? Some people have their devotional period about the same way they have breakfast. They grab a piece of toast and run. How is your spiritual breakfast?

There is no reason for us failing to know the love of Christ, because God can do for us what is exceeding abundantly above all that we ask or think. It is God's power that produces this in us.

Most of us would admire the church at Ephesus because of their activity and their defense of the faith. They tested men who came in their midst and said they were apostles and expelled them when they found them lacking.

Judas would not have found any reason to criticize this church either. They were not expending their efforts in devotion to Christ. Judas criticized Mary because of her love for the Saviour. She bathed His feet with her tears and His head with expensive ointment, and this latter Judas considered a waste. But the Lord Jesus Himself pointed out the root problem as being a lack of this very devotion which Mary so much exemplified.

Ephesus and Thessalonica

There is a striking comparison between the church at Ephesus and the church of Thessalonica. Paul, in writing to the Thessalonians, commented on their work of faith, their labor of love, and their patience of hope. But the Lord Jesus, in commenting on the church of Ephesus, said that He knew their works, their labor, and their patience. There is a marked difference here.

The Lord could not say of Ephesus "I know your work of faith." They worked but what they did was not the result of faith. Their Christian activity did not result from a faith which is produced by being in the Word: "Faith cometh by hearing, and hearing by the word of God" (Rom. 10:17).

In Ephesus they labored but it was not a labor of love. When love is gone then work is labor and toil. These Ephesians were an energetic people for the Lord, but their emphasis was upon what they were doing, not upon their love for Christ. The same can be true of us. We can be busy day and and night going to all kinds of church arranged programs and activities, good in themselves, but devoid of love so far as our own hearts are concerned, if our actions are not motivated by our love for Christ.

The Thessalonians had patience of hope, but in Ephesus there was just patience. Hope was gone. All they had left was endurance. When love is in the heart and hope is present then we can patiently wait as we labor for the return of the Lord and the joy of seeing Him and being rewarded at His hand.

Paul speaks of the presence of this same love in Romans 5. He says, "And not only so, but we glory in tribulations also: knowing that tribulation worketh patience; And patience, experience; and experience, hope; And hope maketh not ashamed; because the love of God is shed abroad in our hearts by the Holy Ghost which is given unto us" (Rom. 5:3-5).

When we are born again from above, the Holy Spirit comes into our lives and brings with Him the whole love of God and pours it out into our hearts. Are we letting that love flow through us? Or have we closed the door on it?

It is so easy to work and labor and have patience and yet have the underlying motive missing. The externalities are there but love is gone. It was Paul who said, "The love of Christ constraineth us." It was this that drew him on to serve the Lord. With this love as the basis of our service we will have works of faith, labors of love and patience of hope.

We need ever to keep before us such passages as I Corinthians 13:1-3: "Though I speak with the tongues of men and of angels, and have not charity [love], I am become as sounding brass, or a tinkling cymbal. And though I have the gift of prophecy, and understand all mysteries, and all knowledge; and though I have all faith, so that I could remove mountains, and have not charity [love], I am nothing. And though I bestow all my goods to feed the poor, and though I give my body to be burned, and have not charity [love], it profiteth me nothing." Then Paul concludes this remarkable chapter by stating: "Now abideth faith, hope, charity [love], these three; but the greatest of these is charity [love]."

Orthodox But Backslidden

Vance Havner once said, "People can be just as straight as a gun barrel theologically, but as empty as a gun barrel spiritually." Our outward conduct and service can be ever so correct and yet at heart we may be backsliding. There can be a zeal for orthodoxy which is in reality unorthodox. This was true in Israel's experience. The Apostle Paul pointed this out when he wrote: "Brethren, my heart's desire and prayer to God for Israel is, that they might be saved. For I bear them record that they have a zeal of God, but not according to knowledge. For they being ignorant of God's righteousness, and going about to establish their own righteousness, have not submitted themselves unto the righteousness of God" (Rom. 10:1-3). This was a zeal for God and for righteousness which was unorthodox because the Israelites did not recognize God's provision through faith.

It is possible for us today to contend for the faith in a way that is in conflict with the faith itself. There can be zeal for denouncing sin and zeal for truth, but if these are not motivated by love for Christ they can narrow down to nothing else but hate.

It is doubtful if any man in Scripture denounced sin more than Jeremiah did. But he was known as the "weeping prophet." The love of God was in Jeremiah's heart and he wept before God and before his captors as he warned those evil men of the consequences of their sins. Zeal not motivated by love is worthless to God.

I wonder if there ever has been a time when people were busier for God than they are right now. Yet with many of them the first love is gone.

Christ warned that in the last days the love of many would wax cold. This does not mean that there would be no more love in the hearts of His people for Him but that the early warmth and compassion of that first love would be gone. Some of us would try to apply these conditions to the liberals in the church, but Christ was speaking of the orthodox, the fundamental, the Bible-believing Christians.

It is possible for a wife to remain loyal to her husband, to have no thought or desire for any other man, yet her first love to her husband may be gone. I've had occasion to counsel with a number of husbands and wives who protested that they dearly loved each other, yet there was so much contention and friction between them that it was evident their first love for each other was no longer there.

The same condition can show up in our church life. Some church members are faithfully present on Sunday mornings and evenings. They are at prayer meeting also; and they are always active with things that need to be done. But it is a matter of orthodox behavior, not love.

We are slighting our Heavenly Bridegroom when we slight this first love. He is coming one of these days to claim His Bride; but are we as members of that Bride preoccupied with other things?

Warning and Counsel

Christ warned the church in Ephesus with a heart of deep compassion for them. He said to them, "Remember therefore from whence thou art fallen, and repent, and do the first works; or else I will come unto thee quickly, and will remove thy candlestick out of his place, except thou repent." There are four words, all beginning with the letter "r," that make it easy for us to remember Christ's words to them. They are: remember, repent, repeat and remove.

Remember

First then, the Lord said, "Remember therefore from whence thou art fallen." The Prodigal Son illustrates this truth for us. He had to come to the end of himself before he remembered. He spent all he had on godless living, then finally came to the place where he would have been glad to eat what he was feeding the hogs. It was then he remembered his father's home, the food he provided and the love he expressed. The Prodigal resolved to return to his father and tell him that he was no more worthy to be called his son, but would be happy to become one of his hired servants. So the son returned. He was seen by his father while still a long way off and was joyfully received back into the home in the position of a son.

The message to you and me in this word to Ephesus is: "Remember your own sinful life. Remember how I saved you from it. Recall those precious honeymoon days when you were first born again." If we could but realize it, what is being touched on here is the most tender aspect of our relationship with the Person of the Lord Jesus Christ. It is the Bridegroom speaking to the Bride. The honeymoon is over and that first love, that something that drew them close together, that which made them do things for each other because they loved each other, is now gone. Love has given place to duty and work and labor. "Remember those days," the Saviour is saying. "Stop for a moment. Think for a moment."

It is important that we take time to think, for we live in such a busy world that we often do not do so. But we must pause in order to reflect on what we are and where we are going and wait upon God for His direction. Let God refresh our souls now as He did in those early honeymoon days when we first came to know Christ.

Repent

In the second place, the Lord said to the church at Ephesus, "Repent." This means to turn back in heart, to turn back in purpose, and to return to the life of love. Why do we serve Him at all? The answer we often give is that He did so much for us we want to do something for Him. Is this our only reason? The Lord cannot accept that kind of labor. Any work or ministry that is not motivated by love He cannot accept, because it is motivated by some carnal purpose within our hearts. We may be ever so sincere and earnest about what we are doing, but unless love is there our work falls short. Paul said that "the love of Christ constraineth us." It is this that returns us to our first love and first works. Faith is also evident for our work springs from belief in Him. We trust Him and therefore work for Him. We have the hope of His coming again and the hope of glory with it. All of these follow in the proper order when love leads the way.

Repeat

How can we repent and repeat or do the first works as the Lord admonishes here? The Old Testament provides an illustration that will help us see this truth. While Israel was in the desert she was given manna as her daily food. But one of the requirements concerning manna was that each person had to go out and pick up the manna every day. It had to be fresh. In this way God gave them a practical lesson on what it means to have fresh contact with Him each day.

How much time do we spend with the Lord each morning? Some of us might answer 15 minutes or 30 minutes in Bible reading and prayer. The next question is, Did we do this because of love for the Lord or as a sense of duty? Did we allow Him to speak to us out of His love letter? Did we converse with Him as with one we love? Are we really still in love with the Lord Jesus Christ? To reestablish that first deep fellowship we must repent and go back and do it the way we did at first. Perhaps the habit will not return to us overnight but we must make a start. Let us do the first works of love again. Lack of love proves lack of faith and loss of confidence in Him. So let us love Him supremely.

Remove

A sad warning then follows in the words, "Or else I will come unto thee quickly, and will remove thy candlestick out of his place." The coming here is not Christ's Second Coming. It is not the Judgment Seat of Christ when He will test our works for rewards. This is a personally supervised judgment that could befall us in our present life.

This is touching upon the most tender aspect of our relationship with Jesus Christ. We, He says, are the apple of His eye and He could not leave us in a condition of heart separation from Him. When a saved person's first love is gone but he keeps being active in Christian things, he is simply serving out of a sense of duty or because of human compassion called forth by the terrible need in those about us. These things are not in themselves wrong, but they are not to be the motivating source of our labor for Christ. Why was it Christ came to help us? Was it out of pity? No, He loved us, and it was this love that caused Him to want to do something for us.

The Lord made the same provision for the members of the apostolic church as He has made for each of us. When we trusted Him as Saviour, He gave us the Holy Spirit and through Him we have the love of God in our hearts. This should be the basis of all service for Him.

The Holy Spirit Himself will not be removed from the believer, but where we are not living up to our responsibilities His power will not be seen in our lives. The Spirit of God is given to us forever and assures us of our salvation, but He may remove from us the power to be light bearers.

The indwelling Holy Spirit witnesses to us concerning Christ and makes Christ's character manifest in us. But He cannot accept our works which are done in the energy of the flesh. The Spirit is in us to energize us for work that will be acceptable to the Lord Jesus Christ. He knows we cannot do the Lord's work of ourselves. We do not have what it takes. Our capacities such as willpower, physical strength and mental ability are good in themselves and the Lord wants to use them, but only to the degree that we love Him.

The Lord said that unless these matters were righted in Ephesus He would remove the lampstand. The lampstand is the church. This is not the building or the organization but the ability of the church to be a living torch or light bearer. This is a sad characteristic of our day. In our own land are many churches that do not have any spiritual light shining from them. People do not see the Christ of God when they see such churches.

According to Ephesians 4 the Lord Jesus gave gifted men to the Church. "He gave some, apostles; and some, prophets; and some, evangelists; and some, pastors and teachers." The purpose was that they would work to the "perfecting of the saints, for the work of the ministry, for the edifying of the body" (vv. 11,12). These would be the light bearers in the midst of the churches; but if these were removed, then no light would shine. What is the church like that we belong to? Is it merely a beautiful building that people can recognize as a church building because of its lovely steeple or bell? Or do people realize that the church to which we belong is a place where Jesus Christ is at home? Why are so few souls saved in some of our churches today? Why is there so much sin among the churches? Why is there so much barrenness of life among church people? Why? Because the first love is gone.

We may be active and faithful in attending meetings. We may even be very busy in calling and visitation, in supporting missions and taking care of our church obligations in our local community, but is this sufficient? According to II Peter 1:3,4 we are told that God has given us everything that pertains to life and godliness. God gave us eternal life in the first place when we trusted Christ. He made us partakers of His divine nature and then provided virtues that we were to add to our lives so that we would not be barren and unfruitful. But if, after all of these provisions are made for us, we do not respond, then our Lord may find it necessary to remove the lampstand from our midst.

Here is how the lampstand is established. Our Lord, knowing He was going home to heaven, promised to send the Holy Spirit. The Holy Spirit came and chose certain men, endued them with special gifts and gave these men as gifts to the church. Through these spiritual men the church is to be brought to be a living witness for Christ, a lampstand in the vicinity Christ has put that group of believers. This is the positive production of the lampstand.

The removal of the lampstand is in reverse order. The Spirit's operation is taken from the church. He no longer works among His people. As a result, if a spiritual man has been given to the church, that man will disappear from the midst. God will take him out and use him in some other place. So many churches want the up-to-date modern men who are better mixers than some of their predecessors, so they let the Spirit-filled preacher go.

In this way the organized church continues but its witness is gone. It still may continue an active program but it does not contribute to bringing men and women to know Christ. Our Lord is not at home in such a place. The fact that the witness has been removed may not be noticed by many, but should we not be more spiritually alert to these matters?

When the Holy Spirit's witness is gone from a group, so is the benefit of His discernment gone. This is why so many cannot see that they are not witnessing as Christ wants them to and that the church is not full of love for Him. The lampstand, the light of the Holy Spirit, can be removed and for lack of spiritual discernment those in the congregation will not know it. In God's sight there is not an assembly there. There may be a large building but that in itself does not make a witness for the Lord. We may speak with the tongues of men and angels but if we do not have love we become as sounding brass or a tinkling cymbal. Though we have the gift of prophecy and understand all mysteries and all knowledge, and though we have all faith so that we could remove mountains and do not have love, we have nothing. Yes, we might even bestow all our goods to feed the poor and give our bodies to be burned; yet, if we do not have love these things profit us nothing. If this is the case with us we will be ashamed before Him at His coming. "Abide in him; that, when he shall appear, we may have confidence, and not be ashamed before him at his coming" (I John 2:28).

Nicolaitanism

One more subject in the letter to the church at Ephesus needs consideration for it is basic to conditions in our present day. Verse 6 reads: "But this thou hast, that thou hatest the deeds of the Nicolaitanes, which I also hate."

Who were these Nicolaitanes? They have been variously identified, but to me the best explanation lies in the meaning of the word "Nicolaitanes" itself. It comes from *nikao* which means "to conquer," and *laos* which means "people." It is from *laos* that we get our word "laity." If this word is used symbolically in this passage, then it has reference to the earliest form or idea of what we call a priestly order or clergy which later on in church history divided people, who had an equal standing in the churches, into priests and laity or clergy and laity. The Ephesians hated this approach and false division between brethren in Christ.

Now it is not wrong for special gifted men to be found in the churches. God placed them there. We have noted on previous occasions here in these studies that God "gave some, apostles; and some, prophets; and some, evangelists; and some, pastors and teachers; For the perfecting of the saints, for the work of the ministry." God called some of His servants to full-time teaching, preaching and leadership in various ways in order to train His people to do His work. But this sin of Nicolaitanism has so laid hold of many Christians down through the centuries that a wrong place was given to their leaders. Today many Christians relegate soul winning to the pastor only, or perhaps to some evangelist. But God's plan is that every member of the Body of Christ should be a witness. God hates this false division among His people. And He commended the Ephesians for also hating it.

At one time David said, "Do not I hate them, O Lord, that hate thee? And am I not grieved with those that rise up against thee? I hate them with perfect hatred: I count them mine enemies" (Ps. 139:21,22). The word "hate" in this context is not used as evil temper or as we would say, "flying off the handle." What David is speaking of is an inward indignation against wrong, an indignation produced by the Holy Spirit.

There were men in other churches in that first century who played the part of subversives in one way or another. John in his Third Epistle wrote, "I wrote unto the church: but Diotrephes, who loveth to have the preeminence among them, receiveth us not. Wherefore, if I come, I will remember his deeds which he doeth, prating against us with malicious words: and not content therewith, neither doth he himself receive the brethren, and forbiddeth them that would, and casteth them out of the church" (III John 9,10). We find just such conditions in our churches today which is heartbreaking indeed.

A comment I read about Nicolaitanism suggests the danger of man-made systems supplanting Christ. It warned that if a victory were not gained regarding the occupancy of Christ's person, Nicolaitanism would result. How disastrously this came to pass. The comment is: "The first-century church, the wondrously best and used, did not heed Christ's first-love warning, though God permitted chastening in the second and third centuries through suffering and martyrdom (pictured by the Smyrna letter); yet that church, as a whole, did not repent regarding the departure from the first love for Jesus Christ. Nicolaitanism came in." How much further that error has progressed through the centuries!

Chapter Six

The Church in Smyrna
(Rev. 2:8-11)

We read concerning Smyrna: "And unto the angel of the
church in Smyrna write: These things saith the first and the
last, which was dead, and is alive; I know thy works, and
tribulation, and poverty, (but thou art rich) and I know the
blasphemy of them which say they are Jews, and are not, but
are the synagogue of Satan. Fear none of those things which
thou shalt suffer: behold, the devil shall cast some of you
into prison, that ye may be tried; and ye shall have
tribulation ten days: be thou faithful unto death, and I will
give thee a crown of life. He that hath an ear, let him hear
what the Spirit saith unto the churches; He that overcometh
shall not be hurt of the second death" (Rev. 2:8-11).

Prophetically, this church represents the period of time
from Nero (A.D. 64) to Constantine (A.D. 316). Nero was
the Roman emperor who began the terrible persecutions
against the church. Constantine protected the church and
made Christianity the state religion, thus uniting the church
and the state.

The passage says that the church at Smyrna would have
tribulation ten days. The word "day" is often used in the
Bible as speaking of certain periods of time such as the Day
of the Lord and the Day of Christ. This apparently is the
thought here for going back over history we find there were
ten periods of severe persecution against the Church at this
time in its history. Three of these were in the first century
beginning with Nero; two were in the second century; and

five were in the third century. This was a time of almost unparalleled suffering for the Church, a time when countless men and women were martyred for their faith.

The following incident comes out of this era of great suffering and shows the caliber of men who were willing to die for their faith in Christ.

"It is written that a king commanding a Christian to recant and give up Christ, said, 'If you don't give up Christ, I will banish you.' The Christian smilingly answered, 'You cannot banish me from Christ; He has said, "I will never leave thee, nor forsake thee." The king then angrily said, 'Well, I will confiscate your property.' The Christian replied, 'My treasures are laid up on high, you cannot get to them.' The king, in greater anger, said, 'Well then, I will kill you.' The Christian answered, 'I have been dead with Christ through this world for 40 years; my life is hid with Christ in God; you cannot touch it.' To which the king said, 'What can you do with such a fanatic?' "

It pays to be that kind of fanatic for the Lord's sake.

The Lord permitted this great time of persecution which lasted for some two centuries. It undoubtedly was permitted because of the spiritual letdown among believers, for they had left their first love. God permits chastening for corrective purposes. This is very clearly stated in Hebrews 12: "For whom the Lord loveth he chasteneth. . . . If ye endure chastening, God dealeth with you as with sons; for what son is he whom the father chasteneth not? But if ye be without chastisement, whereof all are partakers, then are ye bastards, and not sons. . . . Now no chastening for the present seemeth to be joyous, but grievous: nevertheless afterward it yieldeth the peaceable fruit of righteousness unto them which are exercised thereby" (vv. 6-11).

Though the Smyrna church stood true, it did not return as a whole to that first experience of first love with Christ.

Many churches and individuals, even though they saw great victories during this time, did not return to their first love. We believe some did but not all.

In speaking to this church the Lord Jesus describes

Himself as the First and the Last, which was dead and is alive. This is indeed a great comfort and consolation to the children of God in their suffering. The Lord will still be there when all the persecutors are gone. Not only that, but all the persecutors will also have to answer to Him for their evil actions.

So there is every reason for us as believers to take courage. This is not a day without persecution. It is very possible that the persecution of Christians in many lands has been worse in these later years than in any preceding century.

But there is something far more shameful among Christians, and this goes on in countries where little or no persecution of a physical nature is carried on against the church. I am speaking of the shameful murdering of character that some Christians indulge in. This is an inexcusable and deplorable condition to exist among God's people, members of the same Body of Christ. All of these things will come to the front at the Judgment Seat of Christ and will be dealt with, for our Lord is not dead but alive. In His hands are the keys or the authority for dealing with all matters pertaining to His people.

Suffering for Christ

What the Lord Jesus Christ says to the church in Smyrna regarding their suffering and persecution is of encouragement to believers at any time. This is especially so when the suffering is for His cause. In the letter to Smyrna the Lord describes Himself as the First and the Last, the One who was dead and is now alive. In this He tells us that He suffered and that suffering ended in death. But now He is alive forevermore.

He did not say that He died as a martyr. He died as our substitute. But out of this comes also the encouragement to us that in suffering there is victory when our suffering is for Christ. The subject of suffering is raised in Revelation 2:9 where the words are: "I know thy works, and tribulation, and poverty, (but thou art rich) and I know the blasphemy of them which say they are Jews, and are not, but are the synagogue of Satan." There is nothing hidden from our Lord. His analysis of the situation is always correct.

The word "tribulation" in this passage is very strong. This is not speaking of the time of the tribulation (Rev. 6-19), but of a particular kind of suffering. They were under the pressure of persecution. It was a very severe test and some of them may have thought they were being tried beyond their ability.

The tribulation spoken of in this passage could be likened to grain being crushed in a stone mill. Or it might be likened to a winepress with the juice forced out of the grapes under great pressure.

Another illustration of this nature comes out of the Psalms. The Lord Jesus spoke of Himself as "a worm, and no man; a reproach of men, and despised of the people" (22:6). This messianic prophecy is referring to the crushing of certain worms from which scarlet dye was extracted. The Lord can enter into the suffering of His people sympathetically for He also has suffered even to the point of death.

His sympathy extended also to their poverty. Many of them suffered the loss of all their possessions. They were stripped bare of any material comfort. They were made beggars because of the persecutions heaped upon them for their faith in Christ.

He understood this and consoled them in their deep trouble. Paul wrote in connection with this side of our Saviour's life in II Corinthians 8:9: "For ye know the grace of our Lord Jesus Christ, that, though he was rich, yet for your sakes he became poor, that ye through his poverty might be rich." The Lord of Glory understands what poverty is. In sharing with His people in their poverty, He became poor by making them rich with the wealth the world cannot comprehend.

This is one reason He says in Matthew 6: "Lay not up for yourselves treasures upon earth, where moth and rust doth corrupt, and where thieves break through and steal: But lay up for yourselves treasures in heaven, where neither moth nor rust doth corrupt, and where thieves do not break through nor steal: For where your treasure is, there will your heart be also" (vv. 19-21).

The Bible teaches us that a man's life does not consist in the abundance of things he possesses. There is another type of inheritance which comes only from the Lord Himself. We learn in I Peter that we have been begotten into a living hope to "an inheritance incorruptible, and undefiled, and that fadeth not away, reserved in heaven for you, Who are kept by the power of God through faith unto salvation ready to be revealed in the last time" (I Pet. 1:4,5).

That our Lord was poor while on this earth cannot be denied. We read: "And a certain scribe came, and said unto him, Master, I will follow thee whithersoever thou goest. And Jesus saith unto him, The foxes have holes, and the birds of the air have nests; but the Son of man hath not where to lay his head" (Matt. 8:19,20).

Isaiah prophesied concerning Him: "For he shall grow up before him as a tender plant, and as a root out of a dry ground: he hath no form nor comeliness; and when we shall see him, there is no beauty that we should desire him. He is despised and rejected of men; a man of sorrows, and acquainted with grief: and we hid as it were our faces from him; he was despised, and we esteemed him not. Surely he hath borne our griefs, and carried our sorrows: yet we did esteem him stricken, smitten of God, and afflicted. But he was wounded for our transgressions, he was bruised for our iniquities: the chastisement of our peace was upon him; and with his stripes we are healed" (Isa. 53:2-5). He knew what it was to be poor in this world's goods and yet to be rich in the things of God.

Pretenders in the Church

Smyrna was another of the churches that was plagued by pretenders. There were men who came among them claiming to be Jews but the Lord Jesus said they were "of the synagogue of Satan." This is God's classification of these men, not man's. In the language of our day we might perhaps say they were of the "church of Satan."

Paul makes it very clear that God distinguishes between those who are merely physical descendants of Abraham, Isaac and Jacob, and those who are believers. Paul wrote, "For he is not a Jew, which is one outwardly; neither is that circumcision, which is outward in the flesh: But he is a Jew, which is one inwardly; and circumcision is that of the heart, in the spirit, and not in the letter; whose praise is not of men, but of God" (Rom. 2:28,29).

What is said here about being a Jew could well be said today about being a Christian. There are many who pretend outwardly to have some kind of relationship to Christ. They may have joined the church and are active in church circles but God would classify them as of the "church of Satan." Such persons are not born again.

There is all the difference in the world between pretenders and those who belong to the Church of the Living God. No one can belong to that Church except he is born again. Jesus told Nicodemus, "Except a man be born again, he cannot see the kingdom of God."

The destiny of the pretender and of the genuine is not the same. The one who blasphemed in Smyrna, claiming to be what he was not, was destined for an eternal hell which God had prepared for the Devil and his angels. The destiny of the believer is heaven with Christ forever. Many of the believers in Smyrna and down through the years have suffered wrongfully. But this all helped prove their character as it can do for us now. Christian character shows up when we can suffer for wrongs we did not commit and yet do it with grace and love controlled by the Spirit of God.

Our tendency under great stress is to give way to the flesh within us and manifest a spirit of self-pity.

Purpose in Suffering

It is well for us to consider how the glory of Christ's character showed through suffering. We read in Philippians:

"Let this mind be in you, which was also in Christ Jesus: Who, being in the form of God, thought it not robbery to be equal with God: But made himself of no reputation, and took upon him the form of a servant, and was made in the likeness of men: And being found in fashion as a man, he humbled himself, and became obedient unto death, even the death of the cross" (2:5-8).

Though a member of the Godhead, Christ set aside His glories for the time being and was made in the likeness of men. And as though that were not enough, He humbled himself even as a man and became obedient to death on the cross, the cruelest of all deaths.

In Revelation 2:10 the Lord comforts His people by saying, "Fear none of those things which thou shalt suffer." He does not promise that there will not be any suffering. He does not promise relief. In fact, He forewarns them that there will be even more persecution to come. His words are, "Behold, the devil shall cast some of you into prison, that ye may be tried; and ye shall have tribulation ten days: be thou faithful unto death, and I will give thee a crown of life" (2:10). As we have seen, there were ten major persecutions during the time in church history pictured by Smyrna.

The Bible does not promise that anyone who trusts in Christ will have an easy road in this world. The Lord Jesus said in John 16:33: "In the world ye shall have tribulation: but be of good cheer; I have overcome the world."

In the Revelation passage the Lord Jesus Christ attributes tribulation and testing to Satan. He said it will be the Devil who will cast the believers into prison and cause them to suffer. Yet such is the grace and power of God that though He allows Satan to test believers severely, He does not forsake His own; He brings them through the testing purer in character and life than when they entered it. This was true of Job who stated, "Though he slay me, yet will I trust in him." In another place he said, "He knoweth the way that I take: when he hath tried me, I shall come forth as gold." This is victory.

Why does God permit Satan to test the children of God?

The answer is given in Revelation 2:10. The faithful ones in Smyrna would be cast into prison and tried. This is the key. Peter said that the "trial of your faith, [is] much more precious than of gold that perisheth."

"All that will live godly in Christ Jesus shall suffer persecution" according to II Timothy 3:12. Why is this? We already have the answer in the case of Job. Such suffering enables us to learn to know Christ better. And we have His promise that we will not be tested above what we are able to bear. I Corinthians 10:13 says, "There hath no temptation taken you but such as is common to man: but God is faithful, who will not suffer you to be tempted above that ye are able; but will with the temptation also make a way to escape, that ye may be able to bear it."

Job bears this out. At the end of his great suffering he said to the Lord: "I have heard of thee by the hearing of my ear: but now mine eye seeth thee, Wherefore I abhor myself, and repent in dust and ashes."

We have wonderful promises in the Word that should see us through such times of testing. Paul wrote, "We know that all things work together for good to them that love God, to them who are the called according to his purpose" (Rom. 8:28). Tribulation is included in the "all things"; and the purpose of everything that the Lord allows to come into our lives is that we might be conformed to the image of His Son (Rom. 8:29).

Peter has a great deal of information to give us by way of an inspired commentary on suffering. He says, "Beloved, think it not strange concerning the fiery trial which is to try you, as though some strange thing happened unto you: But rejoice." Can a believer actually rejoice in times of testing? Indeed we can when this further information is given us: "Inasmuch as ye are partakers of Christ's sufferings; that, when his glory shall be revealed, ye may be glad also with exceeding joy. If ye be reproached for the name of Christ, happy are ye; for the spirit of glory and of God resteth upon you: on their part he is evil spoken of, but on your part he is glorified." Then he adds this word of warning: "But let none of you suffer as a murderer, or as a thief, or as an evildoer, or as a busybody in other men's matters. Yet if any man suffer as a Christian, let him not be ashamed; but let him glorify God on this behalf. . . . Wherefore let them that suffer according to the will of God commit the keeping of their souls to him in well doing, as unto a faithful Creator" (I Pet. 4:12-19).

There is help in the time of suffering and God works His purposes in us through such suffering. Then, as was promised the believers in Smyrna, those who are faithful unto death will receive from Christ the crown of life.

We need then to be fully convinced or, in other words, to have faith in God's faithfulness. We could say it another way, that we must have the deep conviction that Christ will ever remain faithful. We will never have reason to doubt it. We can always depend upon Him. So if we are faithful unto death, we will not rely on self-courage but, letting Christ be our courage, we will not falter. Then from Him we will receive the crown of life.

The crown of life does not refer to eternal life, for these Christians already had eternal life. The crown believers receive is a victor's crown and, as a result, we will reign with Christ. If we suffer with Him we shall reign with Him, and if we deny Him in the time of suffering He will deny us the privilege of reigning. The subject of overcomers will be taken up later in detail, but suffice it to say here that we are told in Revelation 3:21 that if we are overcomers we will sit with Him on His throne. So the crown given will be a victor's crown, but it will also be a royal crown in the sense that we will reign with Him.

Christ's crown of thorns will be replaced with God's crown of life for us. We shall be victorious, yes, more than conquerors. All of this reflects back to Him who was dead and is now alive. We have nothing to fear when we trust in Him. We will not be hurt of the second death because Christ passed through the portals of death and now lives forever and indwells us who trust in Him. He is able to give us victory in suffering no matter how severe that suffering may be.

Chapter Seven

The Church of Pergamos
(Rev. 2:12-17)

The third church addressed was in Pergamos, a city in John's day which was a center of idol worship. In its prophetic aspect Pergamos covers the Church Age from about the year 300 through the fifth century, with some features that continue on to the end of the Church Age.

The first portion of the letter to Pergamos reads: "And to the angel of the church in Pergamos write; These things saith he which hath the sharp sword with two edges; I know thy works, and where thou dwellest, even where Satan's seat is: and thou holdest fast my name, and hast not denied my faith, even in those days wherein Antipas was my faithful martyr, who was slain among you, where Satan dwelleth" (Rev. 2:12,13).

As we have already stated, Pergamos was the center of idol worship. Some of the things worshiped were nature, medicine and science. Significantly enough the symbol of their worship was the serpent. It is no wonder our Lord designated Pergamos as the place "where Satan's seat is."

We are not without our idolatry today. We live, at least in North America, in a world of wealth and fashion. Mammon has become our god. We hear this so often that it is commonplace to us. It goes in one ear and out the other; but our treatment of the truth of this idolatry does not remove the fact that the materialistic mind captivates most people in our civilization today.

Even among Christians there is a tendency to serve God only as it is convenient for us to do so.

Some of us who lived through the depression have tried to tell our children what things were like at that time. I remember that even as a young pastor I helped support myself by shoveling sand all day for $1.00. Persons who did not live during those years just cannot comprehend such a situation. A dollar means little or nothing to them today. And, of course, it buys a good deal less than it did back in the depression years. There are still many low income families in our country; but the average person looks around to see how the other fellow is living, then becomes worried if his own income doesn't equal or exceed his neighbor's.

There are many Christians who believe that Christianity must not interfere with the world. Yet at the same time they allow the world to dictate to Christianity all it wants to. If a new style comes along many Christians will follow it without question as to its modesty. If the world adopts new methods of doing things, some Christians feel they have to go along with them—unconcerned whether they are harmful. Still many Christians resist the thought of Christianity influencing the world. The idea of separation of church and state becomes nothing more than having Christianity in the church and confining it there, not allowing its influence to spread.

This attitude is illustrated by what a businessman said who was being talked to about letting Christ influence all his life. This man's answer was, "I want you to know that I don't mix my religion with my business." This is the same as saying that he did not want to have Christ as the preeminent One in his life. How many of us think this way?

I read of a man who in his application for work, gave the pastor of his church and his Sunday school teacher as references. He was asked to get a reference from someone who had worked with him during the week. The personnel manager wanted to know how this man rated in his work and attitudes during the week, not just on Sunday. Many Christians want to live their lives in tight compartments, keeping God and the church for one area of life and not letting His teaching and life permeate their secular contacts.

Constantine, the Roman emperor during the first part of the prophetic aspect of Pergamos, did the very opposite of what we have been considering. He made Christianity the state religion, but he did not do it in the way God wanted it done. It is true that the nation that forgets God will soon find God dealing with it. On the other hand, God does not approve of the marriage of church and state, that they become one, with the inevitable result that the state supports and controls the church.

Sharp Twoedged Sword

The Lord describes Himself to Pergamos as the One who has the "sharp sword with two edges" (2:12). In Revelation 19:15 Christ is spoken of as having a sword going out of His mouth. We know this is symbolic. What it teaches us is that we need to remember when He speaks He speaks with power as the Executive of the universe. The sword is the Word of God and is twoedged in that with it the Lord has power to convict all men and to convert those who believe. On the other hand, He has the power to condemn the person who refuses His authority and rejects His Word.

We know from Hebrews 4:12 that the Word of God is lifegiving. It distinguishes between the soul and spirit and even discerns the thoughts and intentions of the heart. When that same Word controls us, under the direction of the Holy Spirit, it enables us also to discern the deeper things of our own nature, our thought life and motives.

Concerning God the Book of Hebrews tells us: "Neither is there any creature that is not manifest in his sight: but all things are naked and opened unto the eyes of him with whom we have to do" (4:13). So it is no wonder that His Word cuts deeply. This is why Paul said, "Preach the word; be instant in season, out of season; reprove, rebuke, exhort with all longsuffering and doctrine" (II Tim. 4:2). The Word of God which is the sword of the Spirit must be used by us if we are to work effectively for the Lord.

The rise and growth of many false cults can be traced to a lack of God's Word in many hearts and minds. People have not studied the Bible as they should and have been easy prey for many of these false teachers.

This same living Word is the word by which God made the heavens and the earth from nothing. He spoke and the heavens and the earth came into being. That same Word will slay the rebels who rise up against Christ. The Lord is sovereign and His Word is sovereign so that what He says stands for time and eternity. Nothing can change it.

This same Word also divides between those who are born from above and those who are not. We are born again by the Word of God which liveth and abideth forever, or we are lost by rejecting it.

Different Kinds of Peace

In Matthew 10:34-36 the Lord said something that has puzzled many people. His words are: "Think not that I am come to send peace on earth: I came not to send peace, but a sword. For I am come to set a man at variance against his father, and the daughter against her mother, and the daughter in law against her mother in law. And a man's foes shall be they of his own household." Then again in Luke 12:51-53 He says: "Suppose ye that I am come to give peace on earth? I tell you, Nay; but rather division: For from henceforth there shall be five in one house divided, three against two, and two against three. The father shall be divided against the son, and the son against the father; the mother against the daughter, and the daughter against the mother; the mother in law against her daughter in law, and the daughter in law against her mother in law."

Let us analyze this matter and see what light the Word of God itself throws on it. Peace is spoken of in the Scriptures in three different ways. First of all there is peace *with* God as we read in Romans 5:1: "Therefore being justified by faith, we have peace with God through our Lord Jesus Christ." Now when Christ said He came not to bring peace but a sword, He was not talking about this kind of peace. The peace described in Romans 5:1 was made through Christ in reconciling us to God. This is the peace which every individual finds who comes to Christ by faith.

There is another kind of peace spoken of in the Bible which is the "peace *of* God." We read in Philippians 4:6,7: "Be careful [anxious] for nothing; but in everything by prayer and supplication with thanksgiving let your requests be made known unto God. And the peace of God, which passeth all understanding, shall keep your hearts and minds through Christ Jesus." This is inward peace which results from the believer having committed everything to God through prayer and supplication with thanksgiving. This results in the peace *of* God protecting the mind and emotions of the believer.

There is a third kind of peace the Bible speaks of and that is "peace on earth." This is the kind of peace the world is seeking today, peace among nations. This is the kind of peace men are talking about at the peace tables. It is also the kind of peace that men are seeking. They even fight wars to try to obtain it. It is universal peace which will come to the nations only when Christ rules on earth.

So what our Lord was telling His listeners, in the passages quoted from Matthew and Luke, was that the truth He was proclaiming concerning His death and resurrection was not at that time going to bring world peace. It would not bring the kingdom age of peace then but rather conflict among men because some would receive Him as Saviour and others would not.

He did leave a legacy of peace, however, for the individual believer. We read in John 14:27: "Peace I leave with you, my peace I give unto you: not as the world giveth, give I unto you. Let not your heart be troubled, neither let it be afraid." So far as wars among the nations are concerned these will continue until Christ comes to bring world peace.

Satan Worship

The Lord Jesus said to the believers in Pergamos that He knew all about the circumstances of their lives. He knew what they faced and the kind of environment they lived in. He said, "I know thy works, and where thou dwellest, even where Satan's seat is" (v. 13). Pergamos apparently was a center of Satan worship.

Satan worship began in Babylon many years ago under Nimrod. Satan's seat or throne was there at that particular time. The so-called mother-child worship began with Nimrod and his wife Semiramis in Babylon many centuries before Christ. All religious movements except true Christianity have some of their beliefs rooted in what began back there in Babylon.

By the time this period of church history prophetically pictured in the letter to Pergamos had arrived, the center of Satan worship had moved to Pergamos. Later the throne of Satan was moved to Rome. The Devil saw that persecution during the Smyrna age had only strengthened the church, so he let up on persecution. He brought in a new era in which the church was assimilated into the state under Constantine. Here Satan operated as an angel of light.

Some Christians today live under Communism or in other areas among people who will not tolerate Christianity. We do not all face the same conditions, but even in our own country to work among ungodly men and women has its peculiar trials. Nevertheless, we have the assurance from our Lord that He knows all about us.

Danger of Premature Judgments

"I know thy works, and where thou dwellest, even where Satan's seat is: and thou holdest fast my name, and hast not denied my faith, even in those days wherein Antipas was my faithful martyr, who was slain among you, where Satan dwelleth" (2:13).

The Lord knows all about our living conditions, the

temptations to which we are exposed and the motives that govern our conduct. He can judge us correctly. This is a factor we must bear in mind with regard to our evaluating another person's actions. We need to know how much the other person has to face and resist before we can be even reasonably accurate in our approving or disapproving of the other person's conduct.

Are we sure that if we would face the same problems in the same environment as the person we tend to criticize that we would do any better than he did? Or it may be that in our case it is easy to run the race because there are few obstacles to hinder us.

Do we realize how easy it is to murder character by simply not knowing the facts about the other person? Our judgment may be harsh whereas our Saviour, knowing the circumstances, would render an entirely different judgment than ours. For lack of adequate knowledge we might even commend a person when there is nothing to commend.

Circumstances can be of a hidden nature such as problems in the home, one's circle of friends, or conditions in the church that few know about. On the other hand the circumstances may be very obvious. They may be outward for all to see.

We must always keep in mind that there are hidden recesses of the heart that only God can know. Few of us know the burdens others may be carrying. There is a great judgment day coming when the Lord Himself will evaluate what we have done in this life for Him. In that judgment (known as the Judgment Seat of Christ, II Cor. 5:10), we will not be judged as to whether we will get to heaven or not. That is not what is in view here. There is no doubt that our Lord, who will be Judge at that time, will reverse many of our quick and unfair judgments. There may be some who will feel ashamed when they see what they really did and were lauded down here. It will be a time when the first may be last and the last, first. Premature judgment is one of the gravest sins that we Christians can commit.

We are admonished in I Corinthians 4:5 not to judge

things ahead of time. We are to leave things until the Lord comes and He will check the motives of men's hearts. Much of present-day criticism among Christians is false because not enough is known of the other person's circumstances.

Satan's Throne

We have previously noted in this letter to Pergamos that Satan's throne was located there during the time of John's ministry. Pergamos was the base for Satan's operations. He is not omnipresent like God. That is, he isn't present everywhere at the same time. Nevertheless he has ability to travel very swiftly between one point and another, one might say with the swiftness of lightning.

He is not all powerful or omnipotent though he retains the power he received when he was first created. He was Lucifer, the greatest of all God's created beings. As far as the Christian is concerned, however, Satan is a defeated foe. When Jesus Christ died on Calvary, He broke Satan's power (Heb. 2:14,15). If we will but recognize that fact and walk in fellowship with Christ, we will be victors in any contest with the Evil One.

Satan is wise but not all-wise. His wisdom is far beyond man's wisdom, but he comes far short of God's omniscience.

Satan has well-organized forces under him. Daniel, for example, was praying and a certain evil angel called "the prince of Persia" interfered for a time with the messenger from God who carried the answer to Daniel's prayer. This prince of Persia is one of the lesser powers that Satan had set over a certain area.

Satan's base of operation, as we have noted, does not remain in the same place indefinitely. It changes from time to time but always to a place that seems to be the most strategic for Satan's particular cause.

In the church of Smyrna Satan veiled his opposition against the church behind the Jewish religious cloak (synagogue of Satan). His strategy did not succeed. The church grew in spite of him. In Pergamos he tried another approach. Instead of persecution he tried to get God's people interested and wrapped up in fleshly things. This included the love of mammon or money. Money itself is not a root of all evil but the love of money is. There is also love of position. It was because of this that many in Pergamos sought popularity through alliances with worldly groups and individuals.

Even in our day, when Satan thinks it is to his advantage, he will resort to open persecution. We have seen much of this in late years. But he will always try to work through the flesh nature wherever possible. The antidote to this is for us to be Christ-centered. We must keep our eyes on the Lord Jesus Christ at all times. Our victory comes when we look away unto Jesus, the Author and Finisher of our faith.

If we become self-centered, Satan will be able to use us to his own advantage. There are large forces in organized Christendom that are seeking the endorsement of the world. They want its approval and whatever popularity it may bring. By this attack Satan has been winning many battles in late years. Whatever or wherever may be Satan's seat of operation today, there is every evidence that he is active with the help of the forces under him throughout the world.

Approval of Pergamos

Two strong notes of approval are given Pergamos. The Lord said to them, "Thou holdest fast my name, and hast not denied my faith" (2:13). Could He say this about us today? Do we hold fast His name? His name has to do with His Person. The church in Pergamos believed Christ was truly God. This was all important in that day as it is in our day. John wrote in his Gospel: "In the beginning was the Word, and the Word was with God, and the Word was God" (John 1:1).

There was a teaching prevalent during the time of Pergamos, and one that has been revived in our day, to the effect that Jesus Christ is a created being, the first and greatest of God's creation. This was and is Satanic teaching.

Our Lord commended the church for holding fast to His

name, believing that He was what He claimed to be. Christ, the Anointed of God, became man through a miracle of the Holy Spirit in the virgin birth. He is eternally God.

John tells us in his Epistles that those who deny that Jesus Christ—the Eternal God—became man, are antichrists. The Apostle wrote: "Beloved, believe not every spirit, but try the spirits whether they are of God: because many false prophets are gone out into the world. Hereby know ye the Spirit of God: Every spirit that confesseth that Jesus Christ is come in the flesh is of God: And every spirit that confesseth not that Jesus Christ is come in the flesh is not of God: and this is that spirit of antichrist" (I John 4:1 3).

In writing to the Corinthians Paul said, "Wherefore I give you to understand, that no man speaking by the Spirit of God calleth Jesus accursed: and that no man can say that Jesus is the Lord, but by the Holy Ghost" (I Cor. 12:3). There is a great need in our day to be careful to discern these spirits. Not everyone who says "Lord, Lord," is of God. Not everyone who does Christian work, even the way we do it, is necessarily of God. We must learn to watch and discern, for Satan is out to deceive.

The other reason for Christ's approval of the church of Pergamos was that they had not denied His faith. The Lord was not talking about *their* faith; He called it *My faith*. There are many obstacles that could hinder your faith and mine but none can hinder Christ's faith. We read in Galatians 2:20: "I am crucified with Christ: nevertheless I live; yet not I, but Christ liveth in me: and the life which I now live in the flesh I live by the faith of the Son of God, who loved me, and gave himself for me." This is more than faith in the Son of God. It is living by His faith. This faith is a gift from God (Eph. 2:8,9) and is produced by the Word of God (Rom. 10:17). This is why we are to continue in the faith, grounded and settled. We are not to be moved from the hope of the gospel.

There may have been times when some of these Christians in Pergamos felt they could not continue to believe. Persecution was too hard. Circumstances made it impossible for them to carry on. But they could still cast themselves upon Him, confessing the weakness of their own faith but accepting His. They were to let Him do the believing through them. Their confidence was in His purpose, in His atoning work, and in His perfecting work.

The emphasis in our day is self-elevation to salvation. Many believe that they will eventually become good enough to be saved.

This same wrong idea carries over into what people think the Christian life is. So many believers think they will become better Christians through self-effort. This cannot be done. We read in Colossians: "As ye have therefore received Christ Jesus the Lord, so walk ye in him" (2:6). We were saved by faith; we are to continue walking by faith.

Complaint Against Pergamos

All was not well at Pergamos. The Lord found some things to commend but He also found some things that were wrong. He said, "But I have a few things against thee, because thou hast there them that hold the doctrine of Balaam, who taught Balac to cast a stumblingblock before the children of Israel, to eat things sacrificed unto idols, and to commit fornication" (2:14).

Not all members of the Pergamos church were guilty of believing and practicing the doctrine of Balaam. Some did, however, and apparently there was no discipline in the church to root out these false teachers or unbelievers from their midst. The church was loyal in the faith but it tolerated false views. It only takes one rotten apple in a barrel to spoil the others. The spiritual life of Pergamos was threatened by the doctrine of Balaam even as the church is threatened by the same teaching today.

What is this doctrine? We need to know, for it is a kind of teaching that Satan has used against the work of God on several occasions.

The historical background concerning this doctrine is found in Numbers, chapters 22 through 25. There we learn that Balaam was hired by Balak, king of Moab, to curse the people of Israel when they passed through the land of Moab on their way to Canaan. Balak was afraid of them and wanted them destroyed. He knew his armies were not strong enough to do the job, so he hired Balaam, a heathen diviner (who, strangely enough, also knew something of the true God), to bring down a curse upon Israel. Balaam tried to earn his ill-gotten wages, but found that instead of cursing Israel he blessed them. God would not allow this evil prophet to curse what He had blessed.

Balaam found that Israel, as a nation, was secure in God's hand. This security rested on God's sovereign will, grace and mercy, which was first revealed to Abraham in Genesis 12. The record is, "I will make of thee a great nation, and I will bless thee." This was an unconditional promise God gave His servant. From one standpoint, then, Israel was immune to Satan's attacks. They were invulnerable to the Enemy's stroke. The final purposes of God in that nation could not be permanently ruined.

But this is only one side of the matter. We must not stop here or we will not see the terribleness of the sin of the doctrine of Balaam. This is the divine record of what transpired when Balaam, instead of cursing Israel, blessed them saying, "How shall I curse, whom God hath not cursed? or how shall I defy, whom the Lord hath not defied? For from the top of the rocks I see him, and from the hills I behold him: lo, the people shall dwell alone, and shall not be reckoned among the nations" (Num. 23:8,9). Again in the same chapter, when Balak rebuked Balaam for blessing instead of cursing, Balaam said, "Rise up, Balak, and hear; hearken unto me, thou son of Zippor: God is not a man, that he should lie; neither the son of man, that he should repent: hath he said, and shall he not do it? or hath he spoken, and shall he not make it good? Behold, I have received commandment to bless: and he hath blessed; and I cannot reverse it. He hath not beheld iniquity in Jacob, neither hath he seen perverseness in Israel: the Lord his God is with him, and the shout of a king is among them" (vv. 18-21). In this fashion God declared Israel's position as a nation before Him and the ultimate purpose He had for them. Balaam and Balak were the emissaries of Satan in this incident, and in dealing with such enemies God declares His ultimate purpose with regard to His people.

In chapter 24 Balaam reiterates the fact that he cannot curse Israel but must bless them and at the same time speak against Moab in so doing. The future glory of Israel's place in the kingdoms of the world is seen in verse 17: "I shall see him, but not now: I shall behold him, but not nigh: there shall come a Star out of Jacob, and a Sceptre shall rise out of Israel, and shall smite the corners of Moab, and destroy all the children of Sheth."

This, as we have said, is only one side of the matter. This relates to God's eternal and sovereign purpose for Israel. He will eventually establish them in their land, and make them His own people, and put His love and commandments into their hearts. No enemy can curse them to the extent that this sovereign purpose of God will be permanently thwarted. His promise to Abraham in Genesis 12 will be literally fulfilled.

Over against this, while they could not be cursed, we find that the nation of Israel suffered for its sins, and individuals in the nation suffered for their sins. The fourth chapter of Deuteronomy contains severe warnings relating to the committing of sin by the Israelites and chapter 28 gives a prophetic picture of their worldwide dispersion due to their national sins.

It is into this phase of Israel's life that the doctrine of Balaam is introduced. Balaam showed Balak how Israel could be temporarily stopped from achieving God's goal. Balak and his people were advised to fraternize with Israel, and to intermarry with them, thus making them ineffective for God's service. This doctrine of Balaam led many of the Israelites to become idolaters and led many to think that because as a nation they were secure in God's sovereign plan, they could sin as they pleased without any adverse effect upon them. This was a false security.

Balaamism Today

It is very apparent from the Scriptures that the doctrine of Balaam is a recurring error. It did great harm in Israel and was a real threat to consecrated living in the church in Pergamos. It is a false view held by many Christians today.

In order to see what is involved here, we must first of all recognize that the Scripture teaches our salvation is secure in Christ. Some, knowing this truth, but either ignoring or being ignorant of other facets of truth related to the subject, take the position that it makes no difference how a Christian lives. If we are safe as Christians, we can mix with the world and won't be hurt by it. If the creed is right, it will make no difference what the conduct is like, they say.

The Bible does teach the sovereign grace of God. It is because of His mercy toward us that there is security in Christ for us. In John 10:28 we read: "And I give unto them eternal life; and they shall never perish, neither shall any man pluck them out of my hand." In the sixth chapter of John's Gospel we read: "All that the Father giveth me shall come unto me; and him that cometh to me I will in no wise cast out" (6:37). These are plain statements of Scripture. There is nothing ambiguous in them.

However, see what John 10:27 says, "My sheep hear my voice, and I know them, and they follow me." If a professed believer is not following the Lord Jesus, it is because he does not belong to Him. The change wrought in the heart through salvation is such that a Christian does not live continuously in sin, but follows Christ.

Proof of this is in I John 3:9: "Whosoever is born of God doth not commit sin; for his seed remaineth in him: and he cannot sin, because he is born of God." There are two very significant statements made here. "Whosoever," we are told, "is born of God doth not commit sin," or better still, "does not practice sin." Then he goes on to say, "For his seed remaineth in him: and he cannot sin." Christ is the seed in us and He cannot sin. The consequence of this is that with

Christ indwelling the believer, the believer can no longer continue practicing sin in the way he did before he was saved.

We still live in flesh bodies and there are times when the fallen nature gets the upper hand. But if living in sin is the continuous characteristic of our lives, then it is evident we do not belong to Christ at all. If there are not evidences of righteousness and godliness in us we are not born of God.

In this same Epistle, John wrote concerning some who had broken their affiliation with God's people. He said of them, "They went out from us, but they were not of us; for if they had been of us, they would ["no doubt" is not in the Greek text] have continued with us: but they went out, that they might be made manifest that they were not all of us" (I John 2:19).

The world and Christ are enemies. There should be no misunderstanding this truth, for James 4:4 says, "Ye adulterers and adulteresses, know ye not that the friendship of the world is enmity with God? whosoever therefore will be a friend of the world is the enemy of God."

The physical fornication that afflicted Israel and portions of the early church is a blot on our civilization today. We have men in the pulpits advocating what they call "the new morality," which is nothing but pagan immorality. Yet some of the clergy in our pulpits are saying immorality is not immorality if there is "love" between the persons involved. There was an attitude of this kind in the Corinthian church, but Paul made it very clear that God does not tolerate sin in His people.

What persecution could not accomplish in Smyrna, Satan accomplished through the doctrine of Balaam in Pergamos. Considering themselves secure in their salvation, some of the members of that church gave themselves over to worldliness and to gross sins of the flesh. They did not realize that security in Christ is not license to sin. This is one of the dangers lying in the ecumenical movement today where doctrinal correctness is avoided and even opposed. Also in the wake of the liberal trends in our churches today is a great moral breakdown such as took place in Israel as the result of

Balaam's teaching. God judged His ancient people for their sins and He is no less exacting among Christians today.

We cannot play with fire and not be burned. Where persecution fails, corruption can succeed.

Nicolaitanism Again

A second charge brought against the church in Pergamos was that they also had some in their midst who believed and practiced "the doctrine of the Nicolaitanes," a doctrine which God said, "I hate." As we saw in the study of the church at Ephesus, the Nicolaitan heresy was possibly the earliest form in the church of the idea of a priestly order that assumed absolute authority over the souls of men. Our Lord taught that he who would be greatest among his people should be their servant. This is a day when man is being exalted, and that exaltation has carried over into our Christian groups. There is much eulogy of the flesh and man-worship where Christ alone should be preeminent. It is easy for us to be dragged into this thing because of the pressure and practices of the day.

God hates the lust for religious power seen in Nicolaitanism. The wrong separation of the clergy from the laity is a great evil in His sight. This tendency was given great impetus when Constantine brought about what might be called the marriage of the church and the state. This produced a form of church government entirely foreign to the New Testament. God gave some apostles, some evangelists, some pastors and some teachers for the perfecting of the saints for the work of the ministry. It is to us who are His saints that God has given the work of the ministry. The spiritual leaders he has appointed are to train the saints to do this work.

We learn from II Corinthians 4:1: "Therefore seeing we have this ministry, as we have received mercy, we faint not." We all have a part in this work for the Lord.

Paul also wrote in II Corinthians: "All things are of God, who hath reconciled us to himself by Jesus Christ, and hath given to us the ministry of reconciliation" (5:18). The spiritual work God wants done is to be done by those who are born again. But the great trend in our day, and its roots can be traced to this old teaching concerning the Nicolaitanes, is to leave all the spiritual work to the clergy. Yet it was all His people that the Lord Jesus commissioned in Acts 1:8: "But ye shall receive power, after that the Holy Ghost is come upon you: and ye shall be witnesses unto me." The early church did not follow through on this immediately. It is not until we come to the eighth chapter of Acts that we read of great persecution against the church which was at Jerusalem. Then it was that the members were all scattered abroad throughout the region of Judea and Samaria. The only ones left in Jerusalem were the Apostles. So the leaders remained in Jerusalem and the others went everywhere preaching the gospel.

Pergamos was told to repent or the Lord would come in personal judgment. They were to turn about from their evil practices, repudiate their wrong and practice the right. Where the Lord said, "I will come unto thee quickly," He was not speaking of His Second Coming but of His personal judgment on the church and those who taught and practiced evil in it. Here again the Word of God was to be employed, for the Saviour said He would "fight against them" with the sword of His mouth.

A little leaven leavens the whole lump. This is a principle that cannot be ignored. A church that tolerates evil teaching and evil people in its midst must expect to receive discipline from God. The only remedy is repentance toward God and repudiation of the evil.

Chapter Eight

The Church in Thyatira
(Rev. 2:18-29)

Like all the other churches addressed in chapters 2 and 3 of Revelation, Thyatira was a local congregation of Christians at the time John wrote. The particular message we have been emphasizing concerning these churches is the period of church history each one represents. Thyatira pictures the church period from around A.D. 500 to 1500, approximately 1000 years. This is the era often spoken of as the "Dark Ages." During this time the church increased greatly in size. Doctrinally it became known as the compromising church and much sin and error were found in it.

False teaching and unscriptural practices that had not been corrected in other churches, or church periods, came to fruition in Thyatira. Much of God's Word was willfully set aside. In various ways, God's Son was supplanted by men. Grievous sins were tolerated and practiced on a wide scale.

In stating that this church set aside God's Word, we do not mean that they threw it into a wastebasket. They robbed the Word of its effectiveness in the hearts of the people by adding tradition and much dogma as a source of truth. Where they used the Word at all, they misinterpreted it to justify some of the false teachings of the church leaders.

The Lord Jesus Christ was set aside as the Head of the church and men were put in His place. So much were sin and the evil practices condoned that the Lord spoke of some in that church as having known the "depths of Satan."

That church was so weakened spiritually that the reformations and revival which followed were not sufficient

116

to bring it back to Christ. Even in our day in which there is so much talk of change in that branch of Christendom that claims the infallibility of man, the leaders have made it very plain that the changes that have been made do not affect the basic structure or doctrinal position of their church.

God has only one answer for apostasy. It is given regarding the judgment God said He would bring on "that woman Jezebel, which calleth herself a prophetess." He said concerning her, "Behold, I will cast her into a bed, and them that commit adultery with her into great tribulation except they repent . . . I will kill her children with death; and all the churches shall know that I am he which searcheth the reins and hearts: and I will give unto every one of you according to your works" (Rev. 2:22,23). So this church, illustrated by a woman and her daughters, will be judged in the way described in Revelation 17.

Jezebel, a name familiar to us from the Old Testament, was a woman who was eventually destroyed by the very government she herself corrupted. This is the kind of thing that will take place in the church at large as pictured in Revelation. It will help corrupt the governments of the world (including our own in the States), and then one day it will be destroyed by these same governments.

With this panoramic view of Thyatira we are now ready to consider the message to that church in greater detail.

Description of Christ

First there is the description of Christ who speaks to the church. "These things saith the Son of God, who hath his eyes like unto a flame of fire, and his feet are like fine brass" (2:18). This repeats a portion of the description of Christ given in chapter 1. There we see Him as He stands at the right hand of the Father, both as High Priest and coming Judge. What He says is spoken with authority and power and finality. His are not empty words. He is all powerful; what He says He can and will do. Some of the world's mightiest nations like to think of themselves as being all powerful, but they fall far short of the power of the Son of God. He has a right to speak, for all things were made by Him and for Him all things consist. Without Him there would be nothing in existence.

We must learn to serve Him with fear and trembling. This is not the kind of fear that we might show were God like Satan and held a whip over us. The fear spoken of here is a reverential fear. We worship God with awe and adoration and love.

Another familiar description of Christ is that His eyes are like a flame of fire. He has intimate knowledge of all things. He knows the profoundest secrets. There can be no mistake in what He says or does. There is nothing hidden from Him. He looks into all hearts and knows the motives and intents of each heart perfectly.

His feet are likened to fine brass. This speaks of coming judgment. For certain things there is no remedy, only judgment. Apostasy, as we have already seen, is one of these. This is borne out by Hebrews 10:26-31: "For if we sin wilfully after that we have received the knowledge of the truth, there remaineth no more sacrifice for sins, But a certain fearful looking for of judgment and fiery indignation, which shall devour the adversaries. . . . For we know him that hath said, Vengeance belongeth unto me, I will recompense, saith the Lord. And again, The Lord shall judge his people. It is a fearful thing to fall into the hands of the living God."

God is not a tyrant, but at the same time too many persons tend to take such warnings as these lightly. God will not tolerate sin. He has made the way of escape both from the penalty of sin and its power. If Christians will not avail themselves of the victory over sin that God has provided, then He will have to discipline them because of their sin. God is showing patience now but we must not be self-deceived. "God is not mocked: for whatsoever a man soweth, that shall he also reap" (Gal. 6:7).

Praise

In every letter but two where the Lord has a complaint to lodge against a church, He first tells them all the good things He knows about them. Thus we read in Revelation 2:19: "I know thy works, and charity [love], and service, and faith, and thy patience, and thy works; and the last to be more than the first." We could well follow our Saviour's example here in praising what is good in others before we try to point out the faults they may have. Some among us not only criticize but go so far as to assassinate the character of another believer, failing to see the good things in that person's life. God never overlooks any good in a believer's life whether there is much or little.

Sodom and Gomorrah are described in the Bible as two of the most wicked cities of ancient times. Yet God would not bring judgment on them until what was good in them was taken out. In this case it was Lot and part of his family.

Even farther back than the judgment on Sodom and Gomorrah was the judgment of the flood. Men became so wicked that God was forced to destroy them, yet before He brought worldwide judgment He made provisions to preserve one man and his family. Noah found grace in the eyes of the Lord.

Even Judas, who betrayed the Lord, was given a chance to repent. If he had repented, God would have saved him. He rejected God's offer.

There were some good people in the church of Thyatira. The Lord knew their works, all the hard work they were doing and the love which was the basis for it, and their faithfulness to Him. He saw all they did even to their giving of a cup of cold water. Some people are quick to spread a great banquet, but they are slow to give just a cup of cold water. The smallest deed of kindness done in our Lord's name will not go unrewarded. There is too much today of the big showy things. Let us remember that God does not overlook the ministry of the little things.

There were those in Thyatira who pleased God with their

patience. They had the capacity for being still and quiet when all around them was turmoil. There were many places in the western world during the Dark Ages that were characterized by violence, constant wars and all the suffering that goes with them. Today things of this nature are found all around the world. The Lord sees those who are patient under such trials and in the face of unsettled conditions.

The Lord commended some in Thyatira because they were hard working and the things they did increased in value. The last things they did were better than the first things.

We might well ask ourselves if we are growing in our spiritual lives. Were the works done after our conversion the greatest works for the Lord? Have we left our first love? Or are we progressing in our Christian lives to where we are more effective in what we do for the Lord as the days go by? Apparently some in Thyatira had come back to their first love and were growing in grace and in the knowledge of Christ.

Complaint

The Lord found some very serious faults in Thyatira. He said, "Notwithstanding I have a few things against thee, because thou sufferest that woman Jezebel, which calleth herself a prophetess, to teach and to seduce my servants to commit fornication, and to eat things sacrificed unto idols" (v. 20). There are other aspects to this complaint, but in reality it is one major complaint. They allowed Jezebel to work her own will in their midst.

Thyatira raised no protest against this woman's presence nor did they seek to stop her evil work. In Ephesus, such a condition would not have been allowed to exist. That was a church that tried those who claimed to be apostles and were not. But in Thyatira this evil woman was tolerated. "Toleration" is a popular word today. It is used in such a way as to make it wrong to expose sin. To expose wrong is to show lack of "love," we are told. This is a misuse and misinterpretation of love.

It is very likely that Jezebel was a member of the church in Thyatira, though not a born-again member. The Lord tells us we are to love the unsaved, but that does not mean that we are to shut our eyes to the wrong they may do or to be unequally yoked with them in church membership. There is a difference between loving a person and being tolerant of them. There are many today who want us to make way for the unbeliever in the church and let such bring in their own ideas of right and wrong.

If we give Satan a chance in this way he will take over. We can see this all around us in church circles. Unbelievers are brought inside the church as members and also as preachers. Then the Christian is told he must be tolerant toward such and their ideas because these persons may eventually be won over to Christ. But this does not work.

The Lord says very clearly in II Corinthians 6:14,17: "Be ye not unequally yoked together with unbelievers: for what fellowship hath righteousness with unrighteousness? and what communion hath light with darkness? . . . Wherefore come out from among them, and be ye separate, saith the Lord, and touch not the unclean thing; and I will receive you." The Apostle James speaks very strongly in his Letter: "Ye adulterers and adulteresses, know ye not that the friendship of the world is enmity with God? whosoever therefore will be a friend of the world is the enemy of God" (4:4). What words can be plainer than these?

Jezebel, Wife of Ahab

Whether Jezebel was the real name of the woman in Thyatira who called herself a prophetess and was leading God's people astray, or if the name is applied symbolically, a parallel is certainly intended between the Old Testament Jezebel and this one in the New.

We learn in the Old Testament that Ahab, king of Israel, married Jezebel, a worshiper of the god, Baal. "And it came to pass, as if it had been a light thing for him to walk in the sins of Jeroboam the son of Nebat, that he took to wife

Jezebel the daughter of Ethbaal king of the Zidonians, and went and served Baal, and worshipped him. And he reared up an altar for Baal in the house of Baal, which he had built in Samaria. And Ahab made a grove [for the worship of nature]; and Ahab did more to provoke the Lord God of Israel to anger than all the kings of Israel that were before him" (I Kings 16:31-33).

Jezebel's influence was spiritually disastrous for Ahab and Israel. She not only was a worshiper of idols herself, but was also a militant promoter of Baal worship. She encouraged her husband to be "broad-minded" about religion. We can almost hear her say, "What difference does it make what one believes? After all, you have your God and I have my god. Let us be broad-minded about this."

Ahab was strongly influenced by Jezebel. Whether or not he was naturally what we call a "henpecked husband," she found ways to influence him so that she actually ruled over him.

She opposed with violence the prophets of God. If it had not been for the intervention of Obadiah she might have succeeded in destroying most, if not all of them.

When Elijah came on the scene, he thought he was the lone survivor of the prophets. Certainly there was no other public voice raised at that time on behalf of the Lord. However, the Lord said there were 7000 others who had not bowed the knee to Baal.

Jezebel attempted to displace God's Word with the words of men; and back of that was the teaching of Baal, which was inspired of demons. A similar condition exists today. Men have more knowledge than they have ever had in known history. So great has been the breakthrough in scientific knowledge that men have gotten to the place where they believe they can displace God and live by their own ideas. The facts of true science do not contradict the Scriptures, but the philosophic reasonings of the scientists often do. So we find men rejecting the Word of God because it does not fit their theories. This is as much spiritual fornication as was the idolatry of Jezebel, Ahab's wife, and of the Jezebel that did so much harm in Thyatira.

It is noteworthy that the Jezebel of the Old Testament corrupted the government, then used the government she had corrupted to oppose God's work. In the end it was that very government that destroyed her. The same end is in view for the Jezebel of Thyatira. When the religious apostasy that began in the early church is traced through to its end as given in Revelation 17, we find that the great religious system which will for a while dominate the world will in turn be destroyed by the governments of the world.

A good woman is one of God's best gifts on earth. An evil woman on the other hand is one of the worst things that could come on the earth. In the Old Testament records of the kings of Israel and Judah, the mothers of these kings are frequently mentioned. And whether the king was good or bad could often be traced to whether his mother was godly or ungodly.

Many godly wives have been responsible in a large measure for the spiritual effectiveness of their husbands' work for the Lord. On the other hand, there have been ungodly wives who have destroyed their husbands' ministries.

Jezebel of Thyatira

In Thyatira, Jezebel claimed to be a prophetess even though she was not one at all. We have some women in our day who claim to have visions and new revelations and they can be very spiritually dangerous. Many of our present-day false cults were established by women who claimed special inspiration and special teaching for our times. They may have claimed to have a key to unlock the Scriptures, or the ability to throw special light on certain passages; or they may have added some deep, hidden philosophy of life which was not known until their particular "ism" discovered it. The Lord calls such things "the deep things of Satan." We need in our day to get back to the Bible and stay with it.

The Apostle Paul, inspired of the Lord, forbade women

to speak in tongues and to prophesy in the congregation. He did not forbid them to speak in tongues as such. His prohibition had to do with a public manifestation of that gift. His words are very explicit in I Corinthians 14:34,35. We can't erase these things from the Scriptures. They are there as part of God's revealed will. "Let your women keep silence in the churches: for it is not permitted unto them to speak; but they are commanded to be under obedience, as also saith the law. And if they will learn any thing, let them ask their husbands at home: for it is a shame for women to speak in the church." It is apparent from other Scriptures, as well as from the immediate context of these verses, that wrong teaching was often injected into the assemblies of God's people because of some women who were easily brought under evil control.

In II Timothy, Paul warns that false teachers will come in the last days, having a form of godliness but denying the power thereof. He describes them as "of this sort are they which creep into houses, and lead captive silly women laden with sins, led away with divers lusts" (II Tim. 3:6).

This is not all the Bible says concerning women. For it has much to say about godly women. They have a special place in God's plans and program. Many of our churches would crumble were it not for the godly women who help carry on the work. During our Lord's earthly ministry there were many women who served Him and also helped His disciples.

Picture of a Godly Woman

As we have already noted there are many godly mothers who have had a profound effect on their children. I read somewhere that when God wishes to make a great man He begins with a mother.

The finest tribute paid to godly women is in Proverbs 31. Here is credit given to women who are the very opposite of the Jezebels of history. "If you can find a truly good wife, she is worth more than precious gems! Her husband can trust

her, and she will richly satisfy his needs. She will not hinder
him, but help him all her life. She finds wool and flax and
busily spins it. She gets up before dawn to prepare breakfast
for her household, and plans the day's work for her servant
girls. She is energetic, a hard worker, And watches for
bargains. She works far into the night! She sews for the poor,
and generously gives to the needy. She has no fear of winter
for her household, for she has made warm clothes for all of
them. Her husband is well known, for he sits in the council
chamber with the other civic leaders. She is a woman of
strength and dignity, and has no fear of old age. When she
speaks, her words are wise, and kindness is the rule for
everything she says. She watches carefully all that goes on
throughout her household, and is never lazy. Her children
stand and bless her; so does her husband. He praises her with
these words: 'There are many fine women in the world, but
you are the best of them all!' Charm can be deceptive and
beauty doesn't last, but a woman who fears and reverences
God shall be greatly praised. Praise her for the many fine
things she does. These good deeds of hers shall bring her
honor and recognition from even the leaders of the nation"
(Prov. 31:10-13,15,17-21,23,25,26-31, *Living Psalms and
Proverbs*).

Judgment on Jezebel

Returning now to the passage in Revelation, we find that
God does not let the teaching of this false prophetess go
unchallenged or unjudged. The words are, "I gave her space
to repent of her fornication; and she repented not" (Rev.
2:21). God calls for separation whereas many false teachings
call for compromise. This was the case of the doctrine of
Balaam. We are not to be unequally yoked with unbelievers.
We are to be in this world but not of it. We are to avoid the
trap that Balaam set for Israel when he had them intermarry
with the people of Moab. We are sent as sheep among wolves
but we are not to join with the wolves. God will check our
desires, our motives, our hearts, our thoughts, our purposes,

for He wants us to keep the line of separation clear. The Lord Jesus ate with sinners and even with some of the modernists of that day, but He never joined them nor compromised with them. Some criticized Him then for what He did as no doubt some would do today were He here.

Elijah called on Ahab to sponsor the great meeting on Mount Carmel. Ahab called the people together, but it was Elijah who was the spokesman for God. He did not compromise even in a small way with Balaamism, but ended by destroying the prophets of Baal. Elijah was yoked to God, not to Ahab.

God said to Jezebel in Thyatira that she needed to repent, which meant she needed to turn an about-face and go back in the right direction. Then He warned that if she would not repent, He would cast her into a bed and them that commit adultery with her into great tribulation. The symbolic significance of a bed of this nature has to do with delusion or deceit. Those who persist in false teaching will themselves be deceived.

Concerning the last days of this age, Paul wrote: "But evil men and seducers shall wax worse and worse, deceiving and being deceived" (II Tim. 3:13). And during the Tribulation, deceit and falsehood will reach a climax in the Man of Sin. Paul says, "Even him, whose coming is after the working of Satan with all power and signs and lying wonders, And with all deceivableness of unrighteousness in them that perish; because they received not the love of the truth, that they might be saved" (II Thess. 2:9,10). They will be lost because they will refuse to love the truth which could save them.

There are people today to whom the following applies: "For this cause God shall send them strong delusion, that they should believe a lie: That they all might be damned who believed not the truth, but had pleasure in unrighteousness" (II Thess. 2:11,12). The judgment on those who persisted in following Jezebel's wrong teaching will be that of being sent into the Great Tribulation.

The unregenerated church members and the unregenerate church as such will be cast into the Tribulation (Rev. 17:17).

But the promise in Revelation 3:10 is that God will keep the born-again members of the church out of the Tribulation.

Jezebel's children will be judged and thus the churches will know that it is Christ who searches the reins and hearts of men. Jezebel's children are those who have followed after her pernicious teaching. Those of this group who are on the earth when the Rapture takes place will go on into the Tribulation. They will not only be unbelievers but false teachers as well.

Part of God's judgment against Jezebel is that He will "kill her children with death; and all the churches shall know that I am he which searcheth the reins and hearts: and I will give unto every one of you according to your works."

Jezebel's children are those offspring of the apostate church which by the end times will have spread around the world. God's judgment on them is that He will cast them into the Tribulation. This will not be something to look forward to but something to dread. The Church, the Bride of Christ, will have an entirely different history. But God's judgment against the false teachers will be so severe that it will be a fact well known.

This was true of the judgment of Jezebel, Ahab's wife. She met her death years after Ahab died, but to the last she was scheming for herself against God.

When Jehu came to Jezreel he called on some of her eunuchs to throw her down from her window and thus she died. A little later Jehu decided that though she was a cursed woman she was nevertheless a king's daughter and should be given an honorable burial. But when his servants went to bury her they found only her skull, feet and hands. She had been eaten by dogs as Elijah the prophet foretold. All Israel was made aware of this terrible judgment.

The Faithful in Thyatira

Thank God, Jezebel and her followers were not all that made up the church in Thyatira. There were others who were true to the Lord. Concerning these the Lord said, "But unto you I say, and unto the rest in Thyatira, as many as have not this doctrine, and which have not known the depths of Satan, as they speak; I will put upon you none other burden" (v. 24). Undoubtedly, the reference to "none other burden" has to do with going into the Tribulation and judgments related to it. This is a wonderful promise to the people in Thyatira who do not follow after Jezebel. They were also admonished, "Hold that fast which thou hast." These were to hold fast to the Word of God which in turn would preserve them from error and instruct them in righteousness.

Today we must ever be careful that we do not follow any of the cults that profess to be from God but are definitely against Him. They always have some portion of truth, but they always have a new revelation. We need to heed what Paul wrote to Timothy: "I charge thee therefore before God, and the Lord Jesus Christ, who shall judge the quick and the dead at his appearing and his kingdom; Preach the word; be instant in season, out of season; reprove, rebuke, exhort with all longsuffering and doctrine. For the time will come when they will not endure sound doctrine; but after their own lusts shall they heap to themselves teachers, having itching ears; And they shall turn away their ears from the truth, and shall be turned unto fables. But watch thou in all things, endure afflictions, do the work of an evangelist, make full proof of thy ministry" (II Tim. 4:1-5).

God has no use for neutrality with regard to Himself. We must heed what the Spirit says to the churches. We must do something about spreading the gospel of our Lord.

Look again at the expression "Hold that fast which thou hast." We have the Word of God and to that we must hold fast. At the same time, when we are faithful in this the Lord will reward us. To the church in Philadelphia the Lord wrote: "Behold, I come quickly: hold that fast which thou hast, that no man take thy crown" (3:11). The word "crown" used in this context refers to a victor's crown, and victors will reign with the Lord.

This brings us to the next thought with regard to Thyatira. In verses 26,27 we read: "And he that overcometh,

And keepeth my works unto the end, to him will I give power over the nations: and he shall rule them with a rod of iron; as the vessels of a potter shall they be broken to shivers: even as I received of my Father." What we are being told here is that the person in Thyatira, and also the person in our own day, who will stand fast to the truth of God and overcome in spite of all the surrounding apostasy, will be given the privilege of ruling with Christ over the nations in His millennial kingdom. In a later chapter we will make a more detailed study of the overcomer.

Chapter Nine

The Church at Sardis
(Rev. 3:1-6)

The church at Sardis is known as the sleeping church. In this letter we have presented for us the full view of the church from the time of the Reformation period on down to our own day.

We have seen in the other churches the spiritual deterioration that increased as time went on. At the time of the Reformation God moved through godly men, to bring the church as a whole back to Himself, to His Word, to His will, to His way and to His Son. The Protestant Reformation resulted from this work of God, but the work of Satan against the church was not entirely reversed. This will become more evident when we study the two divergent elements in the church as seen in the churches of Philadelphia and Laodicea.

In discussing this picture of the church as presented in the letter to Sardis we are considering the church not locally or nationally but internationally. In addition, we want to get this worldwide view of the church from the time of the Reformation up to and through our own day.

We learn from this letter that the spiritual impetus given the church in the Protestant Reformation gradually declined until the Lord had to say to Sardis: "Thou hast a name that thou livest, and art dead." This is a terrible indictment and speaks of the spiritual deadness of the church.

During His public ministry the Lord Jesus Christ aptly illustrated the particular kind of condition we find in the organized church today. He said: "When the unclean spirit is gone out of a man, he walketh through dry places, seeking rest, and findeth none. Then he saith, I will return into my house from whence I came out; and when he is come, he findeth it empty, swept, and garnished. Then goeth he, and taketh with himself seven other spirits more wicked than himself, and they enter in and dwell there: and the last state of that man is worse than the first. Even so shall it be also unto this wicked generation" (Matt. 12:43-45).

The Lord was using the illustration of a man who had been demon possessed and then was freed through the demon being cast out. But this man did not fill the vacuum in his life with Christ. So, when the demon returned looking for a place to dwell, he brought seven others with him. There was nothing to keep them from possessing the man again; consequently, his last state was worse than his first.

Let us apply this to the period of church history we are now considering. Toward the end of the Dark Ages there were many protests lodged against the character and claims of the Western Church. Out of this finally came the Protestant Reformation, but deterioration followed as Protestants divided over incidentals instead of letting Christ be preeminent. There were individual churches and individual Christians that grew and developed in spiritual things but Protestantism as a whole declined spiritually and a spiritual vacuum was left.

Protestantism's strong protest against error and corruption was weakened by its failure to possess the fullness of truth concerning the Lord Jesus Christ. He is the life of the church just as He is also the life of the individual Christian. He should have been given absolute possession of the church for He is its rightful Head. When He fills this place, there is no spiritual vacuum that would give place to Satan and the evil forces under him. But where Christ was not given His rightful place, Satan with his powers of darkness moved in and the last state was worse for the church than at the first.

There was plenty of religious activity in Sardis but it was the kind of activity that displaced Christ. Again there was a

compromise with the world as seen in the establishing of
state churches. This made membership in the church a matter
of physical birthright rather than through the new birth. This
led to the idea that a child born to Christian parents
automatically was a Christian. As the years went by this filled
the church and often the pulpit with unbelievers.

Protestantism Today

How much of Protestantism today knows in practical
experience the truth of justification by faith which was the
Bible doctrine upon which Protestantism was founded? This
is a truth that has been lost to vast areas of organized
Christendom. The Reformation began well but later
deteriorated into different religious systems which our Lord
describes as being spiritually dead and lifeless.

In our own day there is a move to unite the different
parts of Christendom. Envisioned is an organic union of all
groups calling themselves Christian. But it is a union of the
flesh and not of the Spirit. According to Ephesians 4:3 there
is a unity of the Spirit which God's people should keep. It is
a unity that exists wherever true believers are found. This,
however, does not necessarily mean organic union. Our
Lord's great prayer for the Church in John 17 is often
appealed to by the members of the ecumenical movement as
Bible support for their program. Here again, the Lord Jesus
was not praying about organizational union but about
spiritual unity.

This period of the church seen prophetically in Sardis
deals with a church that has great enlightenment and much
outward activity. It can point to histories of ministry and
activity for Christ and to creeds that have had many good
things in them. But the sad fact is that, on the whole,
organized Christendom has a name that it lives but it actually
is spiritually dead.

The opening verse in this letter reads: "And unto the
angel of the church in Sardis write; These things saith he that
hath the seven Spirits of God, and the seven stars; I know thy

works, that thou hast a name that thou livest, and art dead" (Rev. 3:1).

Once again we find our Lord presenting Himself as speaker. In this situation He says He has the seven Spirits of God and the seven stars. The expression "the seven Spirits of God" is a reference to the Holy Spirit in His sevenfold completeness. The key to this, as we have previously noted, is in Isaiah 11:1,2: "And there shall come forth a rod out of the stem of Jesse, and a Branch shall grow out of his roots: And the spirit of the Lord shall rest upon him, the spirit of wisdom and understanding, the spirit of counsel and might, the spirit of knowledge and of the fear of the Lord."

The "seven Spirits of God" refer to the Holy Spirit, the Third Person in the Trinity. Though the subject of the Holy Spirit is not as clearly revealed in the Old Testament as in the New, it is nevertheless found there. For example, in the Tabernacle in the wilderness there was a piece of furniture in the Holy Place called the candlestick or lampstand. This was made of gold with a central shaft from which projected three branches on each side, all rising as high as the central shaft. These six branches and the central shaft formed a single unit of seven branches, all ending in sockets into which the seven lamps were placed. This candlestick or lampstand is symbolic of the Holy Spirit.

The Spirit of God is represented first of all by the central shaft. Then the six branches which are knit into it complete the picture of the sevenfold characteristics of the one Holy Spirit. He indwells each individual believer today in this sevenfold manner. The Bible tells us that the Spirit of God is in each one of us who has trusted in Christ (I Cor. 6:19). In the believer and the true Church the Holy Spirit is the lampstand.

A review of this truth which we dealt with briefly in our study of chapter 1 of Revelation will be of benefit at this point.

The Holy Spirit is called the Spirit of wisdom. This refers to His ability to judge soundly, having infinite perception and discernment. He is also the Spirit of understanding, having the ability to comprehend, to interpret or explain clearly. He is also the Spirit of counsel who can help us in our need. He will give us of the truth from the Word that will fit our condition. He is also the Spirit of might since He is all-powerful. There is nothing that can stop Him. He is the all-powerful Spirit by which the Lord Jesus created the universe. The Holy Spirit is also the Spirit of knowledge, meaning He is fully acquainted with all facets of the truth. He is also the Spirit of the fear of the Lord, that is, He produces in us true reverence for the Lord. He is in any true church as the lampstand, but He will be removed from that church if He is constantly resisted or ignored (cf. Rev. 2:5).

No Commendation

There is no person who can speak to our hearts as the Lord Jesus can. If He finds it necessary to reprimand us, He comes first with love and compassion that we, by the grace of God, should seek to follow after. He is not a tyrant waiting to judge us harshly if we do not follow His leading. He wants us to be like Him, and He indwells us to be our very life so that we can be like Him.

In writing to Sardis He says, "I know thy works, that thou hast a name that thou livest, and art dead" (3:1). There is no commendation here. He does not praise them. In the letters to the other churches when He uses the phrase, "I know thy works," He follows it with praise for the good things the church was doing. But there is something seriously wrong here in Sardis. This is a sad and startling complaint to come from the lips of our Lord.

The church at Sardis had plenty of works just as we see many churches today with plenty of activity. We often speak of an active church as a live-wire organization, because we are so conditioned to relate activity to life. Some churches boast of having the best preacher in town because he is able to mix with all kinds of people. Then they often point to their involvement in the social issues of their area which makes them popular among certain people. But man looks on the outward appearance. God looks on the heart.

Sardis, though an active church, was a dead church. And the Lord had to say of them, "I have not found thy works perfect before God" (3:2). Someone may protest and say, "Does God expect us to be perfect?" The word "perfect" is not used here with the thought of absence of any flaws. It means complete, perfect, satisfactory. Their works were none of these. They did not meet God's requirements. The outward observance of religion in the church at Sardis may have been good in the eyes of men, but it was not satisfactory to the heart of Christ. Activity as seen in this church is not wrong in itself. It is this imperfect activity Christ is talking about.

What About Us?

Let us apply this truth to the present day. The Lord does not mention in this letter all that we will speak of here, but they are included in the principle involved. He might well ask us when we have the breaking of the bread at Communion service, do we at the same time feed upon Him? We have what we call our worship services, but do we really worship? Is there an inner communion with Him or do we merely go through the form? We have a set program of hymn singing, Scripture reading, special music and finally the preacher brings a message. But is our worship real?

Some of the hymns and gospel songs we sing we know by memory, but do we actually know and meditate upon their true message? We may follow the practice of Bible reading, but as we read is there any communion with our Lord? I personally advocate that every Christian should read his Bible through at least once a year. But do we read it as a love letter from the One we love? When I am away from home I look forward to receiving letters from my wife. I do not merely read the words but find in the correspondence a oneness and fellowship with her.

What about our giving to the Lord's work? We may give

regularly, but do we do it out of a sense of duty or because we love the Lord? We should give to our local church if our church is preaching the gospel. But is our giving an expression of our heart's adoration for the Lord? If not, that gift is not being registered in heaven. Whether our gift is large or small, if it is given on the basis of mere duty it does not count with the Lord. He weighs the motives of the individual heart.

How about our prayer lives? We may attend prayer meetings, but do we reach heaven when we pray? Are our prayers just a number of sentences strung together to sound like prayer? When we leave prayer meetings where we have joined with other believers, do we leave with the consciousness of having communed with our Lord?

What do we receive from the music in our church services? Perhaps the songs are well chosen, the choir numbers well executed—in fact, the whole musical program of the service may have been pleasant to our ears, but was there real worship in it? Was the harmony we enjoyed so much also appreciated in heaven?

Then what about our church committee meetings? Do they produce the spiritual fruit they should?

There may be many plans and programs in our church life, but are they causing us to grow into the likeness of Christ? Are we developing a compassion for souls?

Do we shrink from suffering for Christ's sake? It may not be physical suffering though it could mean that, but are we willing to face suffering for His sake?

We want our church to be well known and highly regarded. We may want our Sunday school to be outstanding in growth and size, but are we willing to make it the spiritual power it should be regardless of the approval or disapproval of others?

Do we fear God more than we do men? Perfect love, we are told, drives out fear. If we have reverential trust in God, we will fear Him in the sense the Bible means.

Are we anxious for our church's reputation? So was the church in Sardis. Such an anxiety has to do with how other neighboring churches regard ours; but what about our reputation in heaven? What about seeking a compliment from the Head of the Church? The Lord had no compliment for Sardis. We can have the outward form of respectability and religious correctness, and yet be spiritually dead.

We may be fundamental, holding to the truth of the Word, and yet lacking real spiritual life.

Wise Counsel

Some very wise counsel was included in this letter to Sardis. The Lord said, "Be watchful, and strengthen the things which remain, that are ready to die: for I have not found thy works perfect before God. Remember therefore how thou hast received and heard, and hold fast, and repent. If therefore thou shalt not watch, I will come on thee as a thief, and thou shalt not know what hour I will come upon thee."

First of all, the Lord said that the church needed to be watchful. They needed to wake up, to become aware of the lack of spiritual life in their midst, or else the Lord would have to come and judge them. God is never mocked. He is never fooled by the outward appearance of the programs and activities of churches. These things do not make an ounce of impression upon Him unless they are genuine.

Thank God that in every denomination and most individual churches today there are those who are true believers. In some places all that may be left of true faith is expressed in reading some of the creeds such as the Apostles' Creed. At times I have preached in churches where liberalism has been allowed to creep in. But in those churches, as in all others in which I preach, I give them the pure Word of God. I do not know anything else to preach. Then after the service is over I have had some of the old-time, faithful members in those churches come to me and say, "What you preached is what we used to hear in this church." This is a sad commentary on conditions in churches today.

The conditions that Ezekiel wrote about in Israel could well be applied today. He said, "And the word of the Lord came unto me, saying, Son of man, prophesy against the shepherds of Israel, prophesy, and say unto them, Thus saith the Lord God unto the shepherds; Woe be to the shepherds of Israel that do feed themselves! should not the shepherds feed the flocks? Ye eat the fat, and ye clothe you with the wool, ye kill them that are fed: but ye feed not the flock. The diseased have ye not strengthened, neither have ye healed that which was sick, neither have ye bound up that which was broken, neither have ye brought again that which was driven away, neither have ye sought that which was lost; but with force and with cruelty have ye ruled them" (Ezek. 34:1-4).

We are living in the same kind of spiritual environment today. No wonder the Lord wrote to Sardis that they should wake up and strengthen the things that remain. Those things were to be established not in the energy of the flesh but in the strength of the Lord and "in the power of his might" (Eph. 6:10).

If a church is dead, what could there be in it that can be made to wake up? We are told that shortly before a person freezes to death, he begins to feel quite warm and very sleepy. If he is not awakened and made to exercise to warm himself up, then he will die. Apparently this was true of some in Sardis.

The forms and ceremonies that made Sardis look as if it were alive were very beautiful. They were attractive but they were void of life.

I remember a saint of God who told me a number of times his experience in just such a church. It was very formal and ritualistic. It had all the trappings of religion. Many a time the man walked down the isle with candles in his hands. But after a while he woke up to the fact that all of these things were merely of an outward nature. There was no life in his church or in what he was doing. He left that church but too late to help his three oldest children. He would tell me, with tears streaming down his cheeks, how they were now outside the fold. His three younger children, however, were gotten out in time, but the loss of the others was heartbreaking.

There are many such who need to be established in the Word and strengthened in their spiritual lives. Let us determine by the grace of God that what we do for the Lord we will do by making Christ preeminent. When we pray, let us seek to contact Him, not just have an emotional feeling. When we come together for worship, let us genuinely worship our Saviour. Let us continue to give but let it be from the heart, not from a mere sense of duty. Continue to sing if God has given you that ability, but let your message be of Christ. Organization is needed in our churches, but let it be organization that is empowered of God.

The following three verses are good tests in this area. The first test is in I Corinthians 10:31: "Whether therefore ye eat, or drink, or whatsoever ye do, do all to the glory of God." Do we do all we do for God's glory?

The second test is found in Ephesians 5:20: "Giving thanks always for all things unto God and the Father in the name of our Lord Jesus Christ." Can we really thank God for everything we do?

The third test is found in Colossians 3:17: "And whatsoever ye do in word or deed, do all in the name of the Lord Jesus, giving thanks to God and the Father by him."

Are we doing all in the name of Jesus Christ? Can you say this is your goal in life? God recognized the outward symbols of Sardis, and does the same with regard to all churches as far as that goes. But Sardis was earthbound. Let us learn from that church not to be satisfied with externals but see to it that the motives and intents of the heart are pleasing to God.

Warning to Sardis

The Lord said to the church at Sardis: "Remember therefore how thou hast received and heard, and hold fast, and repent. If therefore thou shalt not watch, I will come on thee as a thief, and thou shalt not know what hour I will come upon thee" (v. 3). The Lord is never hasty in His judgments. He is never tyrannical in His attitudes. He is longsuffering and merciful. His patience is infinite. At the same time, God will not be mocked. There are conditions among His people that He will not let continue.

In reminding His people at Sardis that He would come as a thief if they did not change their ways, Christ was not speaking of His Second Coming. He was speaking of a present judgment upon them by which He would remove something valuable from their midst.

He warned the church at Ephesus that unless they repented and did their first works He would come quickly and remove the candlestick from their midst (2:5). He warned Pergamos that unless they changed their ways He would come and fight against them with the sword of His mouth (2:16). Now to Sardis the warning is for them to "watch.' They were to be awake and alert in order to meet their responsibilities or else they would reap the consequences of their neglect.

They needed to stay awake to witness the power of Christ in their midst. They had no guarantee that He would always visit them with power.

We have the same problem today. Many in our churches do not realize that the Holy Spirit is visiting us with power and that we must appropriate that power while it is available. It was ignorance of this very fact that was so disastrous for Israel in the day of our Lord's ministry. We read in Luke 19:41-44: "And when he was come near [to the city of Jerusalem], he beheld the city, and wept over it, Saying, If thou hadst known, even thou, at least in this thy day, the things which belong unto thy peace! but now they are hid from thine eyes. For the days shall come upon thee, that thine enemies shall cast a trench about thee, and compass thee round, and keep thee in on every side, And shall lay thee even with the ground, and thy children within thee; and they shall not leave in thee one stone upon another; because thou knewest not the time of thy visitation." They failed to recognize the time of their visitation by Christ and this ignorance was fatal.

So the warning is to be watchful, a warning that is as much for us today as it was for Sardis in John's day. The things which remain and are ready to die must be strengthened. We must wake up to reality, examine the conditions and seek to remedy them in the wisdom and power of the Lord. This is not only a message for the church as a whole but for each individual in the church.

When a thief comes he comes to take only that which is valuable. So the Lord's warning is that unless we face reality and do things in the power of the Holy Spirit instead of our own strength, He will remove His Spirit from us. This is true for every group that ignores or rejects Him.

God will not accept an imitation. If our Christianity is not in demonstration of the Spirit and of power, His power will be removed. The Lord knows we cannot demonstrate true Christianity in our own strength. Nevertheless, many are trying to do so and, of course, are missing it.

The Lord Jesus Christ has given Himself to us, and the Holy Spirit is working out the life of Christ in us. But when we turn from this, the only alternative God has is to remove His power from us.

There is too much playing church today. The Lord will allow this playing to continue, but He will remove effective power from such groups. Some are building great buildings which produce a show of power. God may leave us with the outward show but minus the inward power. This is what Christ's warning of coming as a thief is all about.

Where is the believer's power of protest today? There was a day in the Western world when it was generally conceded that Sunday belonged to the church. Sunday morning, afternoon and evening were all part of the day of rest and of service for the Lord. Even when radio and later, television came into being, they recognized this fact. But the organized church has failed to live up to its privilege and responsibilities. The world with its amusements has taken over Sunday. Religion in most places is relegated to Sunday morning and amusement to Sunday afternoon and Sunday evening. This is the way many radio and TV stations regard it.

The reason is that we have lost our power of protest. We are making no spiritual impact on the world around us as a whole. We have our programs and make plans for world betterment but that impact from the Holy Spirit living within the believer is largely lost. That is why protest is gone.

Christ's warning to come as a thief in the night reminds us that the person being robbed does not know when the thief will come. The thief comes, takes what he wants and his victim often does not know until later that the thief has been there. However, God warns us. This no criminal ever does. Why is it the Supreme Court and others are robbing our nation of its Christian character in many ways? We criticize the Court for this but our protest seems to be powerless.

We may think that this message to Sardis applies to some other church than the one we belong to. But God is speaking to the fundamental church of today, the Bible-believing church. He is speaking to the fundamental believer. There is a drift among today's orthodox to be doctrinally correct but spiritually ineffective. This is not true of all churches true to the Bible. But we know it is possible to be active for the Lord and yet be spiritually dead in His sight. Remember that when the power of God left Samson, Samson didn't know it.

A Few Faithful Ones

Thank God, what we have just been considering did not characterize all who belonged to the church in Sardis. These words of commendation were given by our Saviour: "Thou hast a few names even in Sardis which have not defiled their garments; and they shall walk with me in white: for they are worthy" (3:4). The Lord knows each individual heart; not one is overlooked. He knows those who are true to Him. He had a spiritual remnant who were faithful to Him in Sardis. God is still in the "remnant business" and always has some He can depend on.

In the prophetic aspect covered by Sardis we find such

men as John Huss, Martin Luther, Savonarola, John Knox, Wycliffe and John Calvin. These are but a few of the better known ones, but there were many others who like them were faithful to the Lord.

Today the same can be said. There are many who have not bowed their knees to Baal; or in the language of this letter to Sardis, many have not "defiled their garments."

When garments are spoken of in a symbolic sense they have reference to character. For example, we read in Isaiah 64:6: "But we are all as an unclean thing, and all our righteousnesses are as filthy rags." The filthy rags in this case speak of a bad character. The same truth is given in Jude 23: "And others save with fear, pulling them out of the fire; hating even the garment spotted by the flesh."

In contrast to this and speaking of those who have not defiled their character, we read in Revelation 19:8 concerning the Bride that it was granted to her "that she should be arrayed in fine linen, clean and white: for the fine linen is the righteousness of saints." In other Scriptures we learn that the robe of righteousness is given to those who are born again. So there should be no misunderstanding what the Lord is saying here when He tells us of those who have not defiled their garments.

The Lord still has His remnant in the world today. The organized church may not recognize this group but what does that matter? If we are approved by Him there will be no reason to be ashamed before Christ at His coming. According to II Timothy 2:12, if we suffer with Christ we will also reign with Him. If we deny Him He will deny us the reigning. Or again, we learn that another path to follow to avoid being ashamed before Him is to study to show ourselves approved unto God, workmen who need not be ashamed, rightly dividing the word of truth (II Tim. 2:15).

We can thank God for this spiritual remnant. What He will do for them while they are still representing Him on earth is made clear in the letter to the church at Philadelphia.

The reward mentioned to these in Sardis who have not defiled their garments is: "They shall walk with me in white:

for they are worthy." On the Mount of Transfiguration the Lord Jesus Christ was so changed before His disciples that they saw Him glowing before them in whiteness of His inner purity. There is actually no comparison to this kind of whiteness with anything we know. The Lord has illustrated our whiteness after cleansing from sin to that of wool and also of snow. But these do not fully describe the whiteness of righteousness that will be the believer's robe.

The Lord is clothed in celestial light as we read in Psalm 104:2: "Who coverest thyself with light as with a garment: who stretchest out the heavens like a curtain." Man was made in the image of God according to Genesis 1:26 and though physically naked they were not ashamed (Gen. 2:25). There was no reason to be, because being made in the image of God they were clothed in the shekinah glory of God. But sin stripped them of this glory, so that we read in chapter 3: "The eyes of them both were opened, and they knew that they were naked; and they sewed fig leaves together, and made themselves aprons" (v. 7). They had reason to be afraid, for sin had come in and the glory of God had departed.

All the creatures of God except man have their natural covering. The covering God intended for man was God's own glory, but this was lost when man sinned. Nevertheless, the new robe provided for us in Christ Jesus will be a glory covering provided by our Lord Himself.

The remnant in Sardis were "worthy." They were not worthy in themselves but were worthy in Jesus Christ. This is described for us in Psalm 24:3-5: "Who shall ascend into the hill of the Lord? or who shall stand in his holy place? He that hath clean hands, and a pure heart; who hath not lifted up his soul unto vanity, nor sworn deceitfully. He shall receive the blessing from the Lord, and righteousness from the God of his salvation." God provides a righteous robe for those who trust in Christ. And such have the assurance that their names will not be blotted out of the Book of Life.

Chapter Ten

The Church in Philadelphia
(Rev. 3:7-13)

This is a very encouraging letter. This church, like all the others addressed in these two chapters, was a local historical church in John's day. But we believe like all the others there was a prophetic aspect in the message given. Philadelphia represents the true church beginning with the missionary church of the last century and continuing on until the Rapture. This letter to Philadelphia is full of promise and strength. I have gone back to it many times for my own personal encouragement.

The Description of the Speaker.

The description of Christ in this letter is confined to one verse. We read: "And to the angel of the church in Philadelphia write; These things saith he that is holy, he that is true, he that hath the key of David, he that openeth, and no man shutteth; and shutteth, and no man openeth" (3:7). Part of the encouragement I receive from reading this letter to Philadelphia is the description given here of Christ. Of course, the whole letter is full of encouragement, for it tells us what God has in store for His children, those who have been born of the Spirit and are following Him.

'He That Is Holy'

First of all, the character of Christ is presented. He is called the One who is holy and true. Nothing can be added to Him as far as His holiness is concerned. No further adjectives

145

are needed to describe the degree of His holiness, for perfect holiness cannot be added to. There is nothing with which to compare His holiness since it is absolute. He Himself is the standard of perfection. He is not only perfectly holy but He is also unchangeably holy. He said of Himself in Malachi 3:6: "I am the Lord, I change not."

God has always been what He is and will always be what He has been. Abraham's God is our God. He has not changed one iota from Abraham's day to ours. As He was then so is He now. Christ cannot be considered less holy than God the Father, for Christ is God.

We have already stated that when we speak of His holiness we are speaking of His character. This has to do with the motives of His heart, the purpose of His mind, and the quality of His thoughts. He is genuine all the way through. His motives are always right, never wrong. They are always good, never evil. What qualities of character do we show? Are we being conformed to the image of God's Son?

'He That Is True'

He not only is holy but He is also true. Holiness speaks of the inward aspect of His character, whereas the fact that He is true speaks of His actions. In other words, what He does is the result of what He is. He is truth itself. This comes from the word meaning "genuine." There are many false messiahs in our day and there will be more in the future. These will succeed in deceiving the apostates, for when men turn from the truth they embrace a lie.

We learn from II Thessalonians 2, beginning with verse 9, that when the Antichrist comes he will deceive many with his lying wonders. Their lack of truth and holiness will make them vulnerable. They will perish because they receive not the love of the truth that they might be saved.

Our Lord said that He came in His Father's name and His own people would not receive Him. Then He predicted that when one would come in his own name, that one would be received. Apparently here He was speaking of the Antichrist.

Paul, in writing to Timothy, told of conditions coming on

the earth because of men's rejection of Christ: "For the time will come when they will not endure sound doctrine; but after their own lusts shall they heap to themselves teachers, having itching ears; And they shall turn away their ears from the truth, and shall be turned unto fables" (II Tim. 4:3,4).

Such deception, however, should not affect the children of God. John says in his First Epistle: "And we know that the Son of God is come, and hath given us an understanding, that we may know him that is true, and we are in him that is true, even in his Son Jesus Christ. This is the true God, and eternal life" (I John 5:20). Our Lord Jesus Christ is true. He is the very personification of truth.

Since He is holy in character and true in His actions, whatever Christ does with individuals or with governments is absolutely true. There is no imperfection in Him. Since He is holy and true He is never unfaithful. He can be depended upon entirely at any time. He cannot be other than what He is.

In the Old Testament He represented Himself as "The Great I AM." When Moses asked in whose name he should say he had come, the Lord said to tell the people that "I AM" had sent him. To interpret this for practical use, we can translate it: "I will be to you what I am." We need to learn to know Him (Phil. 3:10) and appropriate to ourselves what we know Him to be—for He dwells in us in all His fullness.

We know that in ourselves we cannot live holy lives. God knows that and has made provision for us by placing His holiness in us. We are not only counted holy in Christ, but Christ living in us will also live His holy life through us.

We find we have the same promise as was given Moses, that the Lord will be unto us what He is. Thus, as we are loyal to our Lord in our communion and our fellowship He is able to work out His life in us. It is more important to be than to do. The doing comes from the being. Righteous actions come from holy characters. And this is possible in us, as we have noted, because Christ says He Himself will come and be this kind of life in us. According to Colossians 2:9,10 this can be realized for "in him dwelleth all the fulness of the

Godhead bodily. And ye are complete in him." So then every good thing we are, we are because we are in Him.

Not only has God put all things under Christ's feet but He has also given Him "to be the head over all things to the church, Which is his body, the fulness of him that filleth all in all" (Eph. 1:22,23). He who fills the universe is also filling His Body, the Church. This further means that He fills each individual member of that Body.

The Key of David

As we turn back to the letter to Philadelphia we read not only that Christ is holy and true but that He also has all authority. The Scripture says, "He has the key of David." Light is thrown on this by what Isaiah said, "And the key of the house of David will I lay upon his shoulder; so he shall open, and none shall shut; and he shall shut, and none shall open" (Isa. 22:22).

Another passage, one often used at Christmastime, teaches the same truth: "For unto us a child is born, unto us a son is given: and the government shall be upon his shoulder: and his name shall be called Wonderful, Counsellor, The mighty God, The everlasting Father, The Prince of Peace. Of the increase of his government and peace there shall be no end, upon the throne of David, and upon his kingdom, to order it, and to establish it with judgment and with justice from henceforth even for ever. The zeal of the Lord of hosts will perform this" (Isa. 9:6,7).

First, the key of authority shall be upon His shoulders and then the government shall rest upon Him also. To turn over a key to someone is symbolically turning over control or authority to that person. If I should be leaving my house for a while and should turn my key over to my neighbor, I would be giving him right of access to my house and perhaps the responsibility to take care of certain matters for me.

The key is the symbol of authority. This is stressed over and over again in Scripture and especially in the Book of the Revelation. For example, in Revelation 9 we learn how the fifth angel sounded and a "star" fell from heaven and to him "was given the key of the bottomless pit" (9:1,2). What was the purpose of this? This angel was given authority to open the pit and when he did there arose a smoke out of it as the smoke of a great furnace. In the first chapter of Revelation the Lord Jesus says, "I . . . have the keys of hell [*hades*] and of death" (v. 18). In the 12th chapter of the Revelation we see how He uses this power of death and hell, this authority that is given to Him. We find Satan, who deceived the whole world, cast out into the earth and his angels cast out with him. Then a loud voice from heaven is heard saying, "Now is come salvation, and strength, and the kingdom of our God, and the power of his Christ." With Satan being cast out, Christ's kingdom and power are in evidence. This kingdom begins with the return of Jesus Christ and runs all the way through the thousand years of His earthly rule until He finally delivers the kingdom over to His Father (I Cor. 15:25-28).

It is because He is holy in character and true and genuine in His actions that He is given the eternal throne of the universe as His right. We learn from the third chapter of Revelation that Christ now sits upon the throne of His Father, but at a later time He will sit upon His own throne. This is His birthright because of who He is and of what He has done. Psalm 2:7-9 says, "I will declare the decree: the Lord hath said unto me, Thou art my Son; this day have I begotten thee. Ask of me, and I shall give thee the heathen for thine inheritance, and the uttermost parts of the earth for thy possession. Thou shalt break them with a rod of iron; thou shalt dash them in pieces like a potter's vessel."

We are well acquainted by now with Philippians 2:9-11 which tells us that Christ has been given a name above every name. He is supreme. He encouraged His Disciples just before His ascension by assuring them that all authority had been given to Him in heaven and in earth. Therefore, they were to go forward preaching the gospel, and He would be with them. He not only has this authority, but He also possesses the power that goes with such authority. He has all power. When He opens a door, no man can shut it. And when He shuts a door, no man can open it. To be sovereign, which He is, He must have all power. He needs this power to perform His purposes. His will is supreme in the universe. He emphasized His sovereignty through Daniel concerning Nebuchadnezzar's experiences. These experiences were ordained by the Lord Himself so that the living might know that God rules in the kingdoms of men and gives the kingdom to whomever He wills.

What the Lord states here to the church in Philadelphia is not a declaration of His ability to perform, but rather a statement of what He will do. If He opens a door no man can shut it. God the Son is in absolute control of all history. When He opens a door all the hosts of hell cannot close it.

With regard to the Church He said He would build it and the gates of hell would not prevail against it (Matt. 16:18). His sovereign power is demonstrated in Pharaoh to whom He said, "Even for this same purpose have I raised thee up, that I might shew my power in thee, and that my name might be declared throughout all the earth" (Rom. 9:17).

Spiritual Union With Christ

Do we realize that according to Ephesians 2:5,6 we have been raised together with Jesus Christ? It does not say that we *will* be raised, though we know there is going to be a resurrection of the physical body in the days to come. But the fact emphasized in these verses is that we *now* have a spiritual resurrection with Jesus Christ. We have been raised with Him and are now indwelt by Him to labor in this world. We are sent forth to minister, not in our strength and ability but in His.

See what the Word has to tell us with regard to our very thought lives which are under attack from so many directions today. "The truth is that, although of course we lead normal human lives, the battle we are fighting is on the spiritual level. The very weapons we use are not those of human warfare but powerful in God's warfare for the destruction of the enemy's strongholds. Our battle is to bring down every deceptive fantasy and every imposing defence that men erect against the true knowledge of God. We even fight to capture every thought until it acknowledges the authority of Christ" (II Cor. 10:3-5, *Phillips*).

There are men today who oppose God and ridicule the idea of God and try to replace His thinking with theirs. But we have the power of prayer and the power of the Word, because Christ indwells us. Thus, we can bring down to nothing these deceptive fantasies and everything that exalts itself against God. We can so enter into this spiritual fight that we make captive every thought until it acknowledges Christ's authority. This is what Christ can do through us.

This is a day of so-called closed doors to missionary enterprises. Russia has built what some have called an iron curtain to keep others out, including God and His truth. Nevertheless God pierces that curtain by radio. China and India and other countries have been putting up their curtains, but these do not frustrate God. He has ways of getting behind these man-made barriers with His Word by radio. New doors are opening—in some cases greater doors than ever—and God tells us He has set these before us and no man can close them.

The Lord has given the Back to the Bible radio ministry the privilege of going through some of these doors today. Even people who are trying to hide the sin in their lives find that God reaches them where they are. It may be in their own homes or in a hotel room, or in an automobile, or in the place they work, but He can and does reach them through radio. Of course, there are other means that He also can and does use.

Some churches have closed their doors to God's truth and will not preach it. But the people of the congregation listen to their radios and are nourished in that way. Not all, by far, who belong to the organized church belong to God. But God has His Church within the church and that true church group is represented by the church of Philadelphia. God's born-again ones make up the believing church of our day and

with all the believers of this age of the church they make up
the beloved Bride of Christ.

Christ Knows All

The Lord said to Philadelphia as He said to the others, "I
know thy works." He has perfect knowledge of all things.
There is no one who could add anything that He does not
know. There is nothing new for Him to know. He is never
surprised. He is never amazed. He knows you and me—all of
us—through and through.

Here is what Isaiah said in this connection: "Who hath
directed the Spirit of the Lord, or being his counsellor hath
taught him? With whom took he counsel, and who instructed
him, and taught him in the path of judgment, and taught him
knowledge, and shewed to him the way of understanding?"
(Isa. 40:13,14). Paul, in contemplating God's knowledge,
utters one of the greatest of Bible benedictions: "O the depth
of the riches both of the wisdom and knowledge of God!
how unsearchable are his judgments, and his ways past
finding out! For who hath known the mind of the Lord? or
who hath been his counsellor? Or who hath first given to
him, and it shall be recompensed unto him again? For of him,
and through him, and to him, are all things: to whom be
glory for ever. Amen" (Rom. 11:33-36).

Read now what the psalmist said in Psalm 139. This is
from the Knox translation which I use here because of some
of the unusual phrases employed. A person living in sin or
outside of Christ would have reason to fear because of what
we read here. But we will not be frightened if we know Christ
as our Saviour and Lord, and are walking in fellowship with
Him.

"Lord, I lie open to thy scrutiny; thou knowest me,
knowest when I sit down and when I rise up again, canst read
my thoughts from far away. Walk I or sleep I, thou canst tell;
no movement of mine but thou art watching it. Before ever
the words are framed on my lips, all my thought is known to
thee . . . Such wisdom as thine is far beyond my reach, no

thought of mine can attain it. Where can I go, then, to take refuge from thy spirit, to hide from thy view? . . . I praise thee for my wondrous fashioning, for all the wonders of thy creation. Of my soul thou hast full knowledge, and this mortal frame had no mysteries for thee, who didst contrive it in secret, devise its pattern, there in the dark recesses of the earth. All my acts thy eyes have seen . . . A riddle, O my God, thy dealings with me, so vast their scope! As well count the sand, as try to fathom them; and, were that skill mine, thy own being still confronts me. . . . Scrutinize me, O God, as thou wilt, and read my heart; put me to the test, and examine my restless thoughts. See if on any false paths my heart is set, and thyself lead me in the ways of old."

Christ is also our wisdom for He has been made unto us wisdom (I Cor. 1:30). He imparts knowledge to us so that we do not lack where such knowledge is needed.

Qualifications for Entering the Open Door

In the five previous letters to the churches the Lord listed the good deeds and qualities of these churches based on His knowledge of them. But in this case He tells them, "I have set before thee an open door, and no man can shut it."

We need to determine who among us qualifies to have this action of our Lord applied to us. Is this a promise to every believer? We would have to say, no, for three qualifications are made with regard to this. These are found in verse 8.

A Minority Group

First of all, He says, "Thou hast a little strength." He speaks then to a minority group, not to a majority group. The world usually measures strength by numbers, but this is not the Lord's method. The Lord deals here with the remnant. It is through remnants among His people that God has done some of His greatest works. We read in Isaiah 1:9 that the Lord would have destroyed Israel like Sodom and Gomorrah had it not been for a remnant, a minority group that stayed true to Him. The Lord started the Church with 12, then there were 120, then on another occasion there were 500. The day of Pentecost saw 3000 added to the Church, but this was still a small number compared to the world at large. In the early foreign ministry of the Church we find Paul and a few associates canvassing the world with the gospel. God apparently has always worked through a minority group.

Church history records that there has been a faithful remnant all the way through. Even in the church during the Dark Ages there were those who were true to our Lord. We recall in the letter to Thyatira our Saviour said, "But unto you I say, and unto the rest of Thyatira, as many as have not this doctrine, and which have not known the depths of Satan, as they speak; I will put upon you none other burden."

Then to Sardis, the church that represented the Reformation time, it was said, "Thou hast a few names even in Sardis which have not defiled their garments; and they shall walk with me in white: for they are worthy."

There is a remnant today that God is using. The organized church counts its millions. This is a constant emphasis of the ecumenical movement. They believe that with such numbers behind them they will have power to open doors that are now shut. But this is not what God says. It is to His remnant, those powerless in themselves, to whom God opens the doors and keeps them from being closed.

Paul said in Philippians 4:13, "I can do all things through Christ which strengtheneth me." Or again we read in II Corinthians 9:8: "God is able to make all grace abound toward you; that ye, always having all sufficiency in all things, may abound to every good work." These are wonderful promises and they rest on the truthfulness and power of God.

Strength for our task does not lie with us. Paul wrote in I Corinthians 1:26: "Look at your own calling as Christians, my brothers. You don't see among you many of the wise (according to this world's judgment) nor many of the ruling class, nor many from the noblest families. But God has

chosen what the world calls foolish to shame the wise; He has
chosen things of little strength and small repute, yes and even
things which have no real existence to explode the
pretensions of the things that are—that no man may boast in
the presence of God" (I Cor. 1:26-29, *Phillips*).

There are some who lay claim to belong to God's
minority group, the very elect. Some of them claim to be the
144,000 of Revelation 7. But the next two qualifications
God has set separate the true from the imitators.

The Word Kept

Two very simple and profound tests can be made to
determine if a minority group is indeed God's believing
remnant today. The tests are in the expressions "thou . . .
hast kept my word," and "thou . . . hast not denied my
name." This minority group for whom God has provided the
open door which no man can shut will be marked by their
total belief in God's Word. When Jesus Christ prayed to His
Father concerning His disciples, He said, "For I have given
unto them the words which thou gavest me; and they have
received them" (John 17:8).

In light of this we should ask ourselves if we are true to
God's Word including both Old and New Testaments. Are we
true to the Person and Word of Christ? Today we find many
shady interpretations of what is meant by the inspiration of
the Scriptures. There are some who say that the Word of God
is inspired if it speaks to you, but if it doesn't speak to you,
it is not inspired. Just how far can men get from the Word of
God?

The Apostle Paul gives us the Bible view of inspiration in
his Second Letter to Timothy. He wrote, "From a child thou
[Timothy] hast known the holy scriptures, which are able to
make thee wise unto salvation through faith which is in
Christ Jesus." Then the Apostle adds, "All scripture is given
by inspiration of God, and is profitable for doctrine, for
reproof, for correction, for instruction in righteousness: That
the man of God may be perfect, throughly furnished unto all
good works" (II Tim. 3:15-17). So we see that all Scripture is

given by inspiration of God whether it speaks to us or not. It does not need our approval or response to make it God's Word. It is God's Word whether we recognize it as such or not.

Then there are shady interpretations concerning what the Bible teaches on creation. What I refer to here is not wrong interpretations from liberals or apostates. They are interpretations from within our own evangelical schools where we have some men teaching a form of theistic evolution. They believe in God and believe that God was the Creator of life but they do not believe man was a special creation of God. They believe man has developed from primitive forms of life to his present position through evolutionary processes.

We can more readily see the danger to the faith when extremists, such as the apostates, attack the Word. In I Timothy, Paul wrote concerning the last days of this age: "Now the Spirit speaketh expressly, that in the latter times some shall depart from the faith, giving heed to seducing spirits, and doctrines of devils [demons]; Speaking lies in hypocrisy; having their conscience seared with a hot iron" (I Tim. 4:1,2).

Satan corrupts the Word. The critics subtract from the Word. Some large sections of organized Christendom add to the Word. The modernists or liberals supplant the Word with their own ideas. Much of Protestantism neglects the Word. The world rejects the Word. The true child of God, on the other hand, loves it. He meditates upon it—all of it. He reads it, desires it, studies it, treasures it, obeys it, and defends it if necessary. This is the minority group that the Lord is speaking to in this letter to Philadelphia.

The Word itself is powerful. Our Lord said in one place: "It is the spirit that quickeneth; the flesh profiteth nothing: the words that I speak unto you, they are spirit, and they are life" (John 6:63). We know from Hebrews 4:12: "The word of God is quick [alive], and powerful, and sharper than any twoedged sword, piercing even to the dividing asunder of soul and spirit, and of the joints and marrow, and is a discerner of the thoughts and intents of the heart."

This is the Word we are to preach. Paul wrote to Timothy: "Preach the word; be instant in season, out of season; reprove, rebuke, exhort with all longsuffering and doctrine" (II Tim. 4:2). Our responsibility is to tell men what God has said. It is God's Word that is true and inspired and profitable.

If we are going to find out what God has promised us, we must go to His Word. And only if we believe that the Bible is God's Word from cover to cover will we accept what He has said. It is only the Word of God which is empowered by the Holy Spirit to regenerate the soul. This is why the promise of the open door cannot be made to others. It is only by giving out His Word that this power will be seen, for James tells us: "Of his own will begat he us with the word of truth" (James 1:18). Peter expresses the same truth when he says, "Being born again, not of corruptible seed, but of incorruptible, by the word of God, which liveth and abideth forever" (I Pet. 1:23).

Christ's Name Honored

Believing the Word of God to be the Word of God is one of the qualifying earmarks of this particular group to which God is referring. Some may pass this test and yet fail to qualify for the promise when the next test is applied. The next statement, "Thou hast not denied my name," marks the crucial difference here.

We have previously noted that in the Bible a name speaks of character. Here, then, is a group that has not in any way denied Christ His rightful titles nor at the same time His rightful place in their lives. This is a test that many in Ephesus could not meet. They were orthodox in their doctrines, but they had left their first love. On the other hand, the Christ-honoring ones had retained their first love, and they exalted Christ's power and affirmed His absolute authority as Lord. They affirmed His name to be above every name and acknowledged His personal authority in their lives.

This narrows down the qualifications to the place where we would find it difficult to say any particular denomination fits these standards. It would have to be narrowed down to individuals who recognize Christ's absolute authority over their personal lives as Lord.

To affirm His name above every name is to acknowledge Him to be the Jehovah of the Old Testament where He said of Himself, "I AM THAT I AM." This means that He will be to us what He is. He gives Himself to us and becomes our life.

In Him alone is life, and He gives this to us when we trust Him. We must personally recognize the fact that to Him was given the name which is above every name, including our own. He has absolute and final authority over us. So it is not enough that we be fundamental or orthodox in our beliefs. We must acknowledge and demonstrate by total surrender that He is our Lord.

To "not deny his name" is to affirm His deity. Furthermore, it means to affirm that Jesus Christ dwells in His people. Paul makes this clear in Colossians 1:27 where he says, "To whom God would make known what is the riches of the glory of this mystery among the Gentiles; which is Christ in you, the hope of glory."

Because this Christ is in us, our labors are not our own but His through us. Paul says in Colossians 1:29: "Whereunto I also labour, striving according to his working, which worketh in me mightily." There was a time in Peter's life when he was confronted with a vision of animals both clean and unclean let down from heaven on a sheet. He was commanded to eat, but because of his religious background he refused. His words are very revealing because they are so contradictory. What he said was, "Not so, Lord." He acknowledged Christ as Lord and yet he would not do what He said. When Christ is really Lord in our lives we put ourselves completely at His disposal. We do what He tells us to do. It is before such obedient persons that He has an open door which no man can close.

There are some who preach another Jesus according to II Corinthians 11:3,4: "But I fear, lest by any means, as the serpent beguiled Eve through his subtilty, so your minds should be corrupted from the simplicity that is in Christ. For if he that cometh preacheth another Jesus, whom we have not preached, or if ye receive another spirit, which ye have not received, or another gospel, which ye have not accepted, ye might well bear with him." What is meant by another Jesus? It is a Jesus other than the one revealed in the Scriptures. It may be an entirely human Jesus, a good man, one who has pointed out a good way for men to travel through life, but His deity is denied. His lordship is ignored.

Now what is the message that the Lord has for this minority group who believes the authority and inspiration of the Scriptures and who gladly bows to Christ's personal lordship? The message for these is: "Behold, I have set before thee an open door, and no man can shut it." We hear so much today, almost too much, about closed doors. We must not overlook the open doors that are before us. We must honor Christ, recognizing that He has absolute control of all history, and that He has been given a name that is above every name. Final authority lies with Him, and full and complete power to accomplish His aims resides in Him. So when He promises that an open door is before us and no one can close it, we should obey Him and enter.

There was a day when Israel, newly released from Egypt, stood at the Red Sea. The sea was before them and the Egyptians behind them, but God opened the sea and the Israelites went through on dry land.

At another time they came to Jordan when it was at flood stage, but God opened it up for them. When they crossed over, they were confronted with the great fortress of Jericho. But God destroyed Jericho before them and opened up the door to the Promised Land.

Opening Hearts' Doors

God also opens doors to the hearts of men and women. We read in Acts 16:14: "And a certain woman named Lydia, a seller of purple, of the city of Thyatira, which worshipped

God, heard us: whose heart the Lord opened, that she attended unto the things which were spoken of Paul." Her heart was open to the gospel because God opened it. No one else could have done it.

The Lord tells us in John 6:44 that no man can come to Him except the Father draw him. God will open the door. It is for us to enter. We know from II Corinthians, chapter 4, that the gospel is hid from those who are blinded by Satan. But God can and will remove the blindness in answer to our faith and prayer.

We can enter the open doors Christ sets before us when we obey His word. For example we read in James 4:6,7: "But he giveth more grace. Wherefore he saith, God resisteth the proud, but giveth grace unto the humble. Submit yourselves therefore to God. Resist the devil, and he will flee from you." Tremendous power is placed at the disposal of us believers when we submit ourselves to God.

God gave Paul an open door to Corinth. He said to the Apostle: "For I am with thee, and no man shall set on thee to hurt thee: for I have much people in this city" (Acts 18:10). So Paul was encouraged to go out in the name of the Lord, assured that his labors would result in the salvation of many individuals.

Now the Lord Jesus not only said that when He opened the door no man could shut it, but He also said that when He closed the door no man could open it. Paul and others with him found this true in their missionary journeys. They had intended to go to a certain portion of Asia but God had other plans for them. "Now when they had gone throughout Phrygia and the region of Galatia, and were forbidden of the Holy Ghost to preach the word in Asia, After they were come to Mysia, they assayed to go into Bithynia: but the Spirit suffered them not. And they passing by Mysia came down to Troas. And a vision appeared to Paul in the night; There stood a man of Macedonia, and prayed him, saying, Come over into Macedonia, and help us" (Acts 16:6-9). According to this the Lord twice closed doors so that Paul could not go through them, but He opened a door into

Europe. Paul entered Europe which God opened to the gospel.

The same principle of the open door is taught in John's Gospel. In His discourse on the shepherd and the sheep the Lord Jesus said, "And when he putteth forth his own sheep, he goeth before them, and the sheep follow him: for they know his voice" (John 10:4). The shepherd went before his sheep because it was his responsibility to open the door for them. It was their responsibility to follow him through the door.

Here we have the Lord Jesus, the Almighty God, taking us by the hand, going before us, opening doors and sending us out.

The idea of the open door lies at the very threshold of our salvation. Our Lord said, "I am the door: by me if any man enter in, he shall be saved, and shall go in and out, and find pasture" (John 10:9). So when it comes to salvation, Christ is the door through which we enter. When it comes to service, He goes before us and opens the doors and empowers us to follow Him and do His work.

Christ Controls History

We have stated a number of times that our Lord is in control of all history. An illustration of this is given in Isaiah with regard to a man named Cyrus. This was a prophecy made long before Cyrus was born. Nations rise and fall but they are never out of God's control. By the time Cyrus would come on the scene as a conqueror, the Babylonians would have already captured the people of Israel and they would have been captives in that Gentile country for 70 years. God promised that at the termination of this captivity He would send His people a deliverer who would make it possible for them to return to their ancient land.

The prophecy reads as follows: "That saith of Cyrus, He is my shepherd, and shall perform all my pleasure: even saying to Jerusalem, Thou shalt be built; and to the temple, Thy foundation shall be laid. Thus saith the Lord to his anointed, to Cyrus, whose right hand I have holden, to subdue nations before him; and I will loose the loins of kings, to open before him the two leaved gates; and the gates shall not be shut" (Isa. 44:28; 45:1).

Cyrus was a leader of the Medes and Persians who subdued nation after nation and finally took the great city of Babylon itself. Its walls were so thick and high men thought it was impossible to take it. But long before it fell God described the method of entrance that the Medo-Persian army would use.

God set the very time when Babylon would fall. We have the record in Daniel 5 where we learn Belshazzar, Nebuchadnezzar's grandson, celebrated with a great feast while the armies of his enemies surrounded the city. It was the very night that this wicked ruler found out he had been weighed in the balances and found wanting that his enemies entered the city, slew him and took over the kingdom.

Concerning Cyrus God also said, "I will go before thee, and make the crooked places straight: I will break in pieces the gates of brass, and cut in sunder the bars of iron: And I will give thee the treasures of darkness, and hidden riches of secret places, that thou mayest know that I, the Lord, which call thee by thy name, am the God of Israel" (Isa. 45:2,3). It was through the decision of Cyrus that the restoration of Jerusalem and Israel became a reality under Ezra and Nehemiah.

Thus, well over a hundred years before he was born, Cyrus was named and his work described so far as it related to God's plans for Israel. This was a door God opened on time as He said He would.

Our Open Doors

The Lord sets the open doors before us but does not push us through them nor pull us through them. A certain responsibility lies with us. We must decide to act on the basis of God's promises. We read in II Peter 3:9: "The Lord is not slack concerning his promise, as some men count slackness;

but is longsuffering to us-ward, not willing that any should perish, but that all should come to repentance." God's longsuffering is extended to us who are His people. He sets open doors before us and as willing subjects under Him we have no other choice but to obey. We must enter by faith as He opens the door.

This is a truth vividly illustrated many places in the Old Testament. One in particular is the incident when Israel under Joshua's leadership came to the Jordan River. It was there God said to Joshua that the priests were to take the Ark and lead the way, then when they stepped into the river it would open up for them. Now the river at that particular time was at flood stage. Yet all that was needed for this "door" to open was obedience on the part of God's people. No sooner had the feet of the priests touched the water of the Jordan than the river parted. The people walked through on dry land.

When Moses and the Israelites stood before the Red Sea, God asked Moses why he was praying about the matter. The Lord told him to go forward. It looked as though the door was closed, but when Moses stretched his rod over the waters they parted. When Moses met his responsibility, the "door" swung wide open. There is a time to pray, then a time to act. It is useless prayer to keep asking when God says, "Go." The faith concerning the open door will become sight or reality when we obey His orders to go through the door.

A familiar passage to us now is II Timothy 4. But look at it from the aspect of the open door. Paul said to his faithful servant: "I charge thee therefore before God, and the Lord Jesus Christ, who shall judge the quick and the dead at his appearing and his kingdom; Preach the word; be instant in season, out of season; reprove, rebuke, exhort with all longsuffering and doctrine. For the time will come when they will not endure sound doctrine; but after their own lusts shall they heap to themselves teachers, having itching ears; And they shall turn away their ears from the truth, and shall be turned unto fables. But watch thou in all things, endure afflictions, do the work of an evangelist, make full proof of thy ministry. For I am now ready to be offered, and the time of my departure is at hand" (II Tim. 4:1-6).

There was an open door before Timothy which he was to enter. Paul had already gone through all the doors God had opened to him, but the same responsibility rests on every servant of God.

Let us put ourselves at our Lord's disposal. He is looking for men and women of faithfulness: those who are full of faith, who believe Him and follow Him. So obedience through faith is necessary here.

Fear and Guilt

There is an open door before us today that we should be entering. We could approach the subject by asking, what is the main issue in the world today? There are many, such as poverty, or in the political realm there is Communism. These, and issues like them, are not the real and basic problem we face. The basic problem lies in the hearts of men and the fears that govern them.

Fear is in men's hearts because sin is in their hearts. There is an emptiness also because man was made for God, but the unsaved man is alienated from God. And man's emptiness leaves him lonely.

He tries many methods to escape this problem, but his devices leave him worse off than he was before.

Man is gripped by the fear of death and he also has a guilt complex which even psychologists and psychiatrists recognize, but only the Bible offers the real solution for it.

Men are sinners and therefore have come short of the glory of God—thus causing the fear of death. Ours is a world of dying, and yet man wants to live. But he wants to live with his guilt burden removed. He tries entertainment, liquor, new religions, even a return to some phase of nominal Christianity, or he will try Communism. This is the day of the hippie and the revolter against the establishment, but this is also a day when more persons are trying suicide because they have not found the answer to their heart condition.

This presents us with a golden opportunity to present what God has given. We know what the need is, and we have the answer. The Lord Jesus Christ is the answer because when He comes into a heart, the load of sin is taken away. When the load of sin is gone, the fear of death is gone. The guilt complex is removed. Loneliness leaves, for who can be lonely with Christ in the heart? There is no longer that empty feeling because the life is filled with God. The burden is lifted. Man is released. He has peace in his soul and genuine hope for the future.

In our particular work God has given us radio to reach people right where they are. It is sad to think that many persons who attend churches are not finding what they need by way of spiritual help. There is religion today without reality. So we must reach people where they are. Radio, as well as literature, can do this. It can reach people right in the mainstream of life whether in the home or in the car or in the shop or in the office—this is an open door which God has set before us. This calls for obedience—and we must enter.

The Synagogue of Satan

The church of Philadelphia, in its prophetic aspect, represents the evangelical, fundamental, Bible-believing church of the last days composed of those who are born again. This is in contrast to the apostate or the professing church which will come into view when we study the church of Laodicea. To this faithful group in Philadelphia the Lord promises: "Behold, I will make them of the synagogue of Satan, which say they are Jews, and are not, but do lie; behold, I will make them to come and worship before thy feet, and to know that I have loved thee" (Rev. 3:9).

The word "synagogue" means "a bringing together" or "a gathering together" of persons, a collection of religious people. The word is used here in a general sense and can mean any who are claiming to be the people of God but actually are not since they constitute a synagogue of Satan.

The word "church" comes from the Greek word *ekklesia*

which means "called out ones." James in Acts 15 gives a good definition of what the Church is. He states, "Simeon hath declared how God at the first did visit the Gentiles, to take out of them a people for his name." God is calling out a people from the midst of the world's masses for His own glory and for the honor of His name. The true Church, then, is composed of those persons who have responded affirmatively to God's offer of salvation.

We have identified the people who are classified as the "synagogue of Satan" only in a general way. In the early church they were a very specific group. Not too surprisingly, their same, unbiblical doctrines are to be found in the church today.

These imposters are first described in the Book of Galatians. Paul, writing to the believers in Galatia, said, "I marvel that ye are so soon removed from him that called you into the grace of Christ unto another gospel: Which is not another; but there be some that trouble you, and would pervert the gospel of Christ. But though we, or an angel from heaven, preach any other gospel unto you than that which we have preached unto you, let him be accursed" (Gal. 1:6-8). These are very strong words, but they describe certain men who claimed to be Christians but were not.

Their wicked leader is identified in Scripture. We read in II Corinthians 11:14,15: "And no marvel; for Satan himself is transformed into an angel of light. Therefore it is no great thing if his ministers also be transformed as the ministers of righteousness; whose end shall be according to their works."

These are actually imitators who claim to be Christians and members of the true Church, but in reality they are opposed to the things of Christ. They often use a Christian vocabulary but attach meanings to the words other than the recognized Christian meaning. This subtle form of opposition to the gospel has persisted all through church history.

Some of these teachers are described in I John 2:22: "Who is a liar but he that denieth that Jesus is the Christ? He is antichrist, that denieth the Father and the Son." If they do not believe that Jesus Christ was virgin-born, that He was sinless, that He was eternally God come into human flesh—if they deny these foundation truths, they are liars and imposters and are designated as antichrists.

In another place, speaking to a religious group, our Lord said, "Ye are of your father the devil" (John 8:44). These men to whom our Lord spoke lived an outwardly righteous life, but the standards were their own and they gave no glory to God for what they did. They were men producing their own brand of righteousness. So the Lord said they were of their father the Devil "and the lusts of your father ye will do. He was a murderer from the beginning, and abode not in the truth, because there is no truth in him. When he speaketh a lie, he speaketh of his own: for he is a liar, and the father of it." These men were leaders of the Jews in our Lord's time, scribes and Pharisees, so this was a stinging indictment of the quality of their religion.

A Spiritual Unity

We see what just such kinds of religious leaders are trying to do today. They are trying to produce a visible unity which is actually a union among the churches of our day, but the unity in it is false. Ephesians 4:3 tells us, "Endeavouring to keep the unity of the Spirit in the bond of peace." There is a unity the Spirit of God has already provided. It is a unity of heart, not of organization. It is more the kind of unity one finds in an organism. Every member of the Body of Christ is in this unity.

It makes no difference what another person may belong to by way of a denomination; if he is trusting in Christ as his personal Saviour, in other words if he is born again, he and I are united in one body, the Body of Jesus Christ: "For by one Spirit are we all baptized into one body, whether we be Jews or Gentiles, whether we be bond or free; and have been all made to drink into one Spirit" (I Cor. 12:13). The church group this person belongs to may even be led by apostate teachers, but that does not change this person's relationship with Christ. Neither have we the right to count only those as

Christians who belong to our particular denomination. We must also realize that many Christians are not sure the Bible teaches separation. Some of them may never even have heard of it. That is another question that is raised later on in the Book of the Revelation.

The promise made to the faithful in Philadelphia is that a day is coming when God will cause these imposters to worship at the feet of the believer. God will then prove to them that His own born-again ones are his own and He will honor them because they have accepted His love.

Christ has been given a name which is above every name and eventually every creature shall bow at His feet. Our identification with Christ provides us with a share in His ruling. We will have a part in judging the world. Moreover we are told that we shall even judge angels (I Cor. 6:2,3).

We learn in Psalm 110:1,2 that the Lord Jesus was to sit at the Father's right hand until His enemies were made His footstool. Since we are heirs of God and joint heirs with Christ (Rom. 3:17), we too may share in that ruling with Him, that is, if we suffer with Him. Our being united to Christ and being one with Him enables us to inherit some of that which He inherits. So if we suffer with Him according to II Timothy 2:12, we shall reign with Him. If we deny Him the suffering, He will deny us the reigning.

So the co-heirs with Christ, the true Church, will one day be found in the place of power. The enemy will be cast down at Christ's feet; and, therefore, will also be humbled before God's people (see also Eph. 1:22,23).

There is no reason why those who are reading these words should miss becoming identified with Christ. This is through salvation, through the acceptance of the gospel which God has provided in Christ. In the first part of I Corinthians 15 we learn that Christ died for our sins according to the Scriptures, and that He was buried and that He rose again according to the Scriptures. If we believe this—not in a merely mental way, but rather showing repentance toward God and faith toward our Lord Jesus

Christ—then this gospel will put us in the place of salvation and also make it possible for us to reign with Christ.

Kept From the Hour of Temptation

A promise is made in Revelation 3:10 that has great significance for God's people today. The Lord said, "Because thou hast kept the word of my patience, I also will keep thee from the hour of temptation, which shall come upon all the world, to try them that dwell upon the earth." The original language of this verse has the article before the word, "temptation," indicating that it is "The Temptation" or "The Testing" that is being referred to, not just any general temptation or testing. The phrase, "which shall come upon all the world, to try them that dwell upon the earth," makes it clear that the time being referred to is the Tribulation. The "word of my patience" emphasizes that it is Christ's patience, not yours or mine. Because we have kept that, we will be kept from the time of the Tribulation.

The promise is: "I also will keep thee from the hour of temptation." The word "from" is important here. Also in the ninth verse the Lord says to His people, "I have loved thee." This is personal and precious. It is truth of a similar nature. His promise is He will keep His own people from the time of trial that is to come on the world.

The word translated "from" is a Greek preposition of two letters, *ek*, which means "out of." It means to be kept away from something.

In the case of Noah we find one who was not kept away from the flood but preserved through it. The promise to the believer in Philadelphia is more like the experience of Enoch who was translated that he should not see death. He was taken out of this world before the flood came.

A special promise is made to Israel with regard to the Tribulation. God says in Jeremiah 30:7: "Alas! for that day is great [day of the Tribulation], so that none is like it: it is even the time of Jacob's trouble, but he shall be saved out of it." Another preposition is used here and signifies that Israel will be "removed from" *the place* where the testing is. In the 12th chapter of the Revelation we will see this very clearly pictured and what it is Israel will be removed from.

However, the promise to those who are born again in this age is that the Lord will keep them not only from the Tribulation or the persecution involved but also from the very scene or time of Tribulation. The promise is that He will keep us from *the hour* of temptation. The Lord does not say whether this is a long period or a short period. He just simply designates it as the time of Tribulation. So the Church will not only be kept from the Tribulation but it will also be kept from the time during which that Tribulation will be exercised.

This period of Tribulation is described in Daniel 12:1: "And at that time shall Michael stand up, the great prince which standeth for the children of thy people: and there shall be a time of trouble, such as never was since there was a nation even to that same time: and at that time thy people shall be delivered, every one that shall be found written in the book."

A further description of this terrible period is given in Matthew 24 beginning with verse 5. The tribulation is further described in the Book of the Revelation, chapters 6 through 19.

The question now arises, how will God keep them from the hour of testing? In Luke 21:36 we read: "Watch ye therefore, and pray always, that ye may be accounted worthy to escape all these things that shall come to pass, and to stand before the Son of man." God will provide a way of escape for His own at that time.

II Thessalonians 2:7,8 says, "For the mystery of iniquity doth already work: only he who now letteth [hindereth] will let [hinder], until he be taken out of the way. And then shall that Wicked be revealed." Who hinders what in this passage? Who keeps iniquity from reaching its peak? Who hinders Satan from having complete control? Who keeps the Tribulation from bursting upon the world? This is done by the Holy Spirit through the Church of our Lord Jesus Christ.

The members of that Body shall be taken away before God can strike in wrath. His method of doing it will be to snatch them away as we read in I Thessalonians 4:16,17: "For the Lord himself shall descend from heaven with a shout, with the voice of the archangel, and with the trump of God: and the dead in Christ shall rise first: Then we which are alive and remain shall be caught up together with them in the clouds, to meet the Lord in the air: and so shall we ever be with the Lord. Wherefore comfort one another with these words."

God's method of delivering His Church is in catching them away or snatching them away from the world. Thus the word *ek* describes very well what will happen to believers through this age. They will be kept "out of" or "away from" not only the trouble itself, but also from the period of trouble.

Reassurance and Caution

Toward the close of His letter to Philadelphia our Lord said, "Behold, I come quickly: hold that fast which thou hast, that no man take thy crown" (Rev. 3:11). Great reassurance to the believer lies in these words: "Behold, I come quickly." The thought is not so much that the Lord would come very soon after this letter was written, but that when He comes, He will come with great speed. The velocity of His coming is in view here. It will be in a moment, in the twinkling of an eye (I Cor. 15:51,52).

We have seen storm clouds that have changed the atmosphere in a very brief time. Suddenly the wind changes, the storm clouds deepen, then the lightning flashes. Thus it will be when He descends from the heavens. He will come very suddenly and there will be no further opportunity for us believers to gain more rewards.

We read in Matthew 24:27: "As the lightning cometh out of the east, and shineth even unto the west; so shall also the coming of the Son of man be." Though this passage is speaking of His coming to the earth, the speed of His coming will be no less when He comes in the clouds to meet His Church in the air (I Thess. 4:13-18).

Following the Rapture of the Church, Christ will unleash the fury of His judgments upon the earth. His own people of this age will be blessed, for they will be caught away into His presence; but all barriers to the Antichrist and his work will then be removed. God's judgments will begin to be felt upon the earth.

Someone has asked why each group in each church period represented by these various churches should be alerted to the coming of Jesus Christ if He wasn't coming until years after some of these periods were ended. We must remember that the Scripture writers did not know it would be centuries before Christ's return for His Church. They knew He could come at any time, and they emphasized this in their writings. It is very important for us to keep in mind that the Lord can come at any time. This produces an attitude of thinking and of action and of expectancy. An habitual outlook toward the Lord's return fosters a spirit of preparedness. This is a most potent aid to santification. If you felt that the Lord might come tomorrow, just what would you do with your life today? Would it not change things for you?

G. Campbell Morgan, a great saint of God of a past generation, said, "I never begin my work without thinking that perhaps He may intrude that work and begin His own. His word to all believing souls is, 'Till I come.' "

There is an urgency in the expression, "Behold, I come quickly." And there is a word of caution in the phrase, "Hold that fast which thou hast" (v. 11). This means that we are to hold on to something with all our might, just as a bulldog holds tenaciously to whatever he decides to hold on to. Some believers are losing their crowns through neglect. So this word of caution is very much needed.

The Believer's Crowns

The subject of crowns is spoken of a good deal in Scripture and especially in the Book of the Revelation. To the faithful in Thyatira the Lord wrote, "But that which ye have already hold fast till I come" (2:25).

Paul had a great expectancy of the Lord's return and wrote to Timothy: "For I am now ready to be offered, and the time of my departure is at hand. I have fought a good fight, I have finished my course, I have kept the faith: Henceforth there is laid up for me a crown of righteousness, which the Lord, the righteous judge, shall give me at that day: and not to me only, but unto all them also that love his appearing" (II Tim. 4:6-8).

The coming of the Lord could be at any time in our lifetime, and it is necessary that we prepare ourselves for it. He will come first of all into the clouds to meet His Church, and all believers of this age will be taken into His presence. Then there will be what is called in the Scriptures the Judgment Seat of Christ, where the believer's works will be evaluated and rewards will be given or lost, depending on the kind of work he has done. Paul writes of this in I Corinthians 3: "Every man's work shall be made manifest: for the day shall declare it, because it shall be revealed by fire; and the fire shall try every man's work of what sort it is. If any man's work abide which he hath built thereupon, he shall receive a reward. If any man's work shall be burned, he shall suffer loss: but he himself shall be saved; yet so as by fire" (vv. 13-15). This gives us reason enough to be very careful to so live that we do not lose the crown awaiting us.

A crown usually speaks of reward with regard to the believer. This in turn has reference to reigning with Christ. We know the Scripture which says, "All that will live godly in Christ Jesus shall suffer persecution" (II Tim. 3:12). If we are among those who live godly in Christ Jesus, in other words, if we let Christ live His life in us and suffer persecution as a result of it, we have this promise: "If we suffer, we shall also reign with him: if we deny him, he also will deny us" (II Tim. 2:12).

Times of trial can unsettle us; but with the many gracious promises in the Word, there is no reason for us to do something that would cause us to lose our crown and therefore our reigning together with Him.

Keeping the Crown

The expression, "that no man take thy crown," could be translated: "that no one take thy crown." This would include our being careful to see that Satan does not get the upper hand. We have a wonderful promise covering this phase of Christian experience also: "Finally, my brethren, be strong in the Lord, and in the power of his might. Put on the whole armour of God, that ye may be able to stand against the wiles of the devil. For we wrestle not against flesh and blood, but against principalities, against powers, against the rulers of the darkness of this world, against spiritual wickedness in high places. Wherefore take unto you the whole armour of God, that ye may be able to withstand in the evil day, and having done all, to stand" (Eph. 6:10-13).

Encouragement is also given in Galatians 6:9 where we are told not to "be weary in well doing: for in due season we shall reap, if we faint not." We are also undergirded by such a promise as I Corinthians 15:58: "Therefore, my beloved brethren, be ye stedfast, unmoveable, always abounding in the work of the Lord, forasmuch as ye know that your labour is not in vain in the Lord."

James, likewise, has something to say along this line: "Be patient therefore, brethren, unto the coming of the Lord. Behold, the husbandman waiteth for the precious fruit of the earth, and hath long patience for it, until he receive the early and latter rain. Be ye also patient; stablish your hearts: for the coming of the Lord draweth nigh" (James 5:7,8).

We recall the promise made to the Church that its members would judge and rule with Jesus Christ. This was a promise made to the faithful in Thyatira: "And he that overcometh, and keepeth my works unto the end, to him will I give power over the nations: And he shall rule them with a rod of iron; as the vessels of a potter shall they be broken to shivers: even as I received of my Father" (2:26,27).

Our Lord made promises directly to the Disciples which also have reference to this same line of truth. In Matthew 19:28 we read: "And Jesus said unto them, Verily I say unto you, That ye which have followed me, in the regeneration when the Son of man shall sit in the throne of his glory [this has to do with His Second Coming and cleansing of the world], ye also shall sit upon twelve thrones, judging the twelve tribes of Israel." In the Gospel of Luke this matter is phrased in these words: "And I appoint unto you a kingdom, as my Father hath appointed unto me; That ye may eat and drink at my table in my kingdom, and sit on thrones judging the twelve tribes of Israel" (Luke 22:29).

It is true that these were special promises spoken explicitly to the 12 Apostles, but we are not left out. The advice to hold on to the crown is not talking about salvation, but of reward in a future kingdom where we shall rule together with Him.

A good illustration of what will take place at the Judgment Seat of Christ is found in Luke 19. There we find a man going to a far country who, before he went, gave talents to different ones of his servants. When he returned he called on them for their reports of what they had done. "Then came the first, saying, Lord, thy pound hath gained ten pounds. And he said unto him, Well, thou good servant: because thou hast been faithful in a very little, have thou authority over ten cities" (vv. 16,17). The record goes on to show that the lord of those servants went right on down the line with them asking for an accounting, and for those deserving reward he gave such. Where none was due he withheld it.

Chapter Eleven

The Church in Laodicea
(Rev. 3:14-22)

The first portion of this letter reads as follows: "And unto the angel of the church of the Laodiceans write; These things saith the Amen, the faithful and true witness, the beginning of the creation of God" (Rev. 3:14).

Let us first of all take a good look at the name, "Laodicea." The word itself means, "the voice of the people." This is in contrast to "the voice of God." This was a church much more interested in what man had to say than what God said.

We must remember that this was a well-known church in John's day and was located in Asia Minor, known to us today as Turkey. The message in these churches that we have been emphasizing has to do with their place in the overall history of the organized church. Laodicea represents the church that came out of the Reformation, but a church that did not stay with the Reformation doctrines. It represents that element in Christianity which substituted formality for truth. There was also an element of carelessness and negligence, with the emphasis shifting to the church (or churchianity) rather than to Christ. This opened the door for all kinds of false doctrines. Some of those in the Laodicean church missed entirely the basic factors concerning Christ and His reason for coming to atone for man's sins. Another characteristic shows up in those who are not outspoken in their opposition to real Christianity, but do not think it has a place in our culture and social life. They relegate their Christianity to a Sunday, or maybe a Sunday and Wednesday, but leave it out the rest of the time. They are not the kind of people the Lord can depend on. Christ has no commendation of any kind for this church of Laodicea. Nevertheless, the people in the Laodicean church are not beyond the compassion of Christ's heart, for He reaches out for them and seeks to win them to Himself.

These people are not ostracized by the Lord. He tells them what the truth is but does not cease reaching out to them. It would be well for us who are fundamentalists and believe in separation to study this letter to learn how to handle those who do not go along with what we stand for. In spite of their rebellion against Him, Christ still loved them and did not go after them as though He would destroy them. God has no pleasure in the death of the wicked. Before He brings judgment He proclaims mercy.

The one outstanding thing that threatened the Laodicean church was its wealth. Concerning Smyrna the Lord said that He knew their "poverty." Philadelphia had but "little strength." But Laodicea boasted of its wealth saying, "I am rich, and increased with goods, and have need of nothing."

The Speaker

The speaker to every church is Christ Himself. As we have seen, He always describes Himself in a way that is in keeping with the vision of Him given in chapter 1, and at the same time in such a way as to fit in with the spiritual needs of each particular church. He had just the right words to fit the condition and needs of each church.

The Amen

To the church in Laodicea, the Lord describes Himself as "the Amen" (3:14). We often use this word without perhaps realizing its real meaning. It is an untranslated Hebrew word meaning that something is established, that something is sure and positive. As a title for Christ it would mean, "I am the Truth." Not that Christ merely teaches the truth or declares to us the truth, but that He is Truth itself. There is a finality

in this. He is the Truth from which there can be no appeal
whatsoever. There are no higher courts that can change His
decision. He holds the last word in the affairs of each life and
of the whole world.

Since He is the Amen, He is the End. Nothing can be
added or taken away from Him. He is Certainty, Finality and
ultimate Authority. No further search for truth is necessary
when He speaks. His words will be successfully contradicted
by none. He has been given a name and a place of authority
above all in the universe. This fact is a wonderful
encouragement for those who are carrying His message of life
to others, but for the Christ-rejectors this spells final doom if
they persist in their rejection of Him.

The True Witness

In the second place, He tells them He is the One who
declares the truth. He is the "true witness" (v. 14).
Concerning Him the writer to the Hebrews said: "God, who
at sundry times and in divers manners spake in time past unto
the fathers by the prophets, Hath in these last days spoken
unto us by his Son, whom he hath appointed heir of all
things, by whom also he made the worlds; Who being the
brightness of his glory, and the express image of his person,
and upholding all things by the word of his power, when he
had by himself purged our sins, sat down on the right hand of
the Majesty on high" (1:1-3).

It is the Son who speaks to Laodicea and who is the true
Witness of God. He witnesses to the fact that He has seen
God, that He has seen God's purpose and that He has
revealed that purpose to us. He withholds no truth. He gives
us all we need for the present and all we need to prepare us
for eternity. There are no tricks, no "small print" as in so
many documents today. What He has to say is out in the
open. All truth that is needed for the saved or the unsaved,
for the obedient Christian or the backsliding Christian, is
there in what He has spoken.

He strips the Laodicean church of all false appearances.
They think they can deceive men, but they cannot deceive

God. There are people attending good, sound, orthodox churches, but that does not mean they go along with the truth of God in their hearts.

Such falsehood the Lord exposes here in the Laodicean church as anywhere else. He neither exaggerates nor minimizes the condition as He finds it.

The Creator

In the third place, Christ speaks of His authority when He says He is "the beginning of the creation of God" (v. 14). This is important for us to remember and state again and again in our day. Where men, such as the atheistic evolutionist, are seeking to build their philosophies on mere chance, we must ever keep before us that Christ is unique and into His hands has been placed all authority.

In keeping with this is Colossians 1:15-18: "Who is the image of the invisible God, the firstborn of every creature: For by him were all things created, that are in heaven, and that are in earth, visible and invisible, whether they be thrones, or dominions, or principalities, or powers: all things were created by him, and for him: And he is before all things, and by him all things consist. And he is the head of the body, the church: who is the beginning, the firstborn from the dead; that in all things he might have the preeminence." This passage reveals Christ as truly God. He is the Master of what He created. He did not create the world and throw it out in space with life upon it to let that life grow and change in any direction it willed. The Lord Jesus Christ is Governor in His own universe.

He speaks with the authority of Prophet, Priest and King, and yet above all other prophets, priests or kings. As Creator His authority is beyond question. All that the eye can see and even that which the human eye cannot see; He is the Creator of it. Whether one looks at the flowers or the landscape or the grandeur and majesty of the mountains or the power of the restless sea, we see that which came from His hand. It may be the rising and setting of the sun or the song of the nightingale; it may be the spring that supplants the winter or the autumn that supplants the summer. They all trace back to Him as the Creator and Cause of them all.

It is this that the atheistic evolutionist tries to shake off. He wants nothing to do with God's authority. But evolution is only one phase of man's thinking today that would eliminate God, if possible, from His universe. Remember, God is not mocked. Whatever a man sows he will also reap. The day God calls for a reckoning, we will find none will dare question Him.

Christ here speaks to a church which is conceited because of its wealth. And placing its emphasis on its wealth it thinks itself independent of Him. His answer to them, however, is such as to bring a blush of shame to them. They were not so great after all. They were not independent of Him. He is "the Amen" who will be there at the conclusion of things as He was at the beginning.

He is the only source of life for any church. Laodicea was indifferent and cool toward Him, but He spoke to them as the One who is the source of life and who has infinite energy and has had such from the beginning. It is this He wants to show the Laodiceans.

The Complaint

We have already seen that there is no compliment for the church at Laodicea, but there is strong and vigorous complaint. This is found in verses 15 through 17.

In His complaint against this church, the Lord Jesus Christ states in brief but pointed phrases the low spiritual level that He sees. The words are: "I know thy works, that thou art neither cold nor hot: I would thou wert cold or hot. So then because thou art lukewarm, and neither cold nor hot, I will spue thee out of my mouth. Because thou sayest, I am rich, and increased with goods, and have need of nothing; and knowest not that thou art wretched, and miserable, and poor, and blind, and naked."

Is Christ speaking to us and the church we belong to in

these words? Regardless of what we think or pretend, Christ knows the actual conditions that exist among us.

This was a church that was neither cold nor hot but lukewarm. This marks the decline throughout these churches which in their composite message give us a picture of the Church Age. In Ephesus they left their first love. In Pergamos they held to the doctrine of Balaam and had in their midst those who taught the doctrine of the Nicolaitanes. The situation worsened in Thyatira because of the presence of Jezebel who called herself a prophetess. Sardis had a name that they lived but were dead. And now in Laodicea the charge is that they are lukewarm. There was no fervent heat of spirituality in this church. There was no final coldness which would speak of indifference if not hostility. In Laodicea there was no enthusiasm, no sense of urgency, no compassion for the souls of men. This was tragic.

In the letter to Laodicea the Lord speaks to the church at large in our day. But we need not think that all that is said here is for the benefit of those who have departed from the faith or who have grown cold in their labors for the Lord. Even the remnant church, the Philadelphian church, will find needed warning and instruction in what Christ has to say to Laodicea.

Laodicea was charged with being lukewarm. The Lord did not say it was cold. Coldness used in this spiritual sense speaks of a church in a spiritually negative condition. There is an utter absence of the warmth of the power of grace or the gospel as such, no profession of faith, no effort at leading the Christian life or seeking a more satisfying Christian experience. Those who are cold care nothing for Christianity. They pay no attention to it. In their coldness they stand aloof from the church and all Christian associations. These same persons live in spiritual deadness because of being enslaved through their carnal natures. They have no regard to the claims of God in their lives and make no attempt to avail themselves of the gospel which the Lord offers them. Such have completely ignored the purpose of God for them. They are in a state of death and also in a state of condemnation.

Until they are touched and animated by the living faith, the wrath of God abides on them.

However, Laodicea was not cold. Unbelievers or pagans are cold to the gospel. They are untouched by Christ and antagonistic toward Him. But Laodicea was a church that claimed Christ, but their response to Him was only lukewarm.

The Lord Jesus, in speaking to the Pharisees, said in John 9:39, "For judgment I am come into this world, that they which see not might see; and that they which see might be made blind." On the surface this sounds contradictory but the solution lies further on. The message continues in verses 40 and 41: "And some of the Pharisees which were with him heard these words, and said unto him, Are we blind also? Jesus said unto them, If ye were blind, ye should have no sin: but now ye say, We see; therefore your sin remaineth."

Here we find the Lord speaking to a religious group of people and saying they were not totally spiritually blind or else the truth would never have come to them. But the very presence of what truth they had laid extra responsibility upon them so their sin remained on them. Though they saw the truth they did not embrace it warmly.

The cold person is the one who has not yet come to the true knowledge of sin nor to the true knowledge of Jesus Christ. But the lukewarm person is guilty of seeing truth but without enthusiastic or glad response.

Biblical Examples

What is intended in the expression "hot"? This, of course, is the opposite of cold. Zacchaeus furnishes us a good illustration in the spiritual realm here. At first he was cold, untouched by the gospel. Then he heard about Jesus and climbed a tree in order to see Him.

Zacchaeus was a tax gatherer who had taken money under false pretenses. It is no wonder he was hated among the Israelites. When Christ showed His love for him, that love touched his hard heart and caused him to burn in his love for

Christ. He came down from the tree and took the Lord to his house and said to Him, "I am going to restore fourfold everything I have taken in a wrong manner." The love of Christ so warmed this tax gatherer's heart that he set about to make restitution as he turned from coldness to become warm, then hot and pliable under the hand of the Saviour.

Then there was Saul of Tarsus. He was bitter and cold toward Christ and the Church at one time. But after seeing Christ he turned from his hatred and persecution and set himself to serve the Lord with a godly zeal and earnestness that has not been equalled by any other.

Moses might be cited as an illustration of the same truth. He filled a very significant place in Egypt and might have remained in that position, even though he was an Israelite and believer in the Lord, had he kept matters quiet. However, so great was his love for the Lord that when the day of decision came he chose to suffer affliction with the people of God rather than enjoy the pleasures of sin for a season. His heart of love made him serve the Lord wholeheartedly. Moses refused to be called the son of Pharaoh's daughter and identified himself with his own people who were slaves.

There are many other such illustrations in the Scriptures and in history of men and women who have forsaken wickedness and turned with a whole heart to the Lord. They became sold out to Christ.

Lukewarm

Laodicea fitted neither the cold nor the hot in spiritual experience. There is hope for the cold person that he will be awakened to sin and righteousness. The person who is on fire for the Saviour is enjoyable to be around. Lukewarmness is another matter.

Because the Laodiceans were neither cold nor hot, the Lord said He would spew them out of His mouth. This state of lukewarmness characterizes much of the church at large today. Even in Bible-believing, fundamental circles there is a tendency toward lukewarmness. There are not too many who are out-and-out for Christ.

Lukewarmness can be a very self-deceiving spiritual state. The lukewarm ones may partially answer the call to the claims of the gospel. They may think it good form to be a Christian. They may marvel at something of God's grace. They may profess to be believers, having been baptized and become members of the church. Some of them may even have confessed Christ as Saviour and fallen into line in service as a duty, but they have not come to the place where they see the Lordship of Jesus Christ.

The Laodiceans had a degree of seriousness. They had the cloak of Christianity but Christ was not Lord to them. There was something greatly lacking among them. Whether all who are described as members of Laodicea are unsaved, we cannot say for sure. But if there were Christians among them they were indifferent to the vital doctrines of the Word of God. So much of what we hear today is that if people are good and virtuous and charitable and kind, they must be real Christians. The whole ecumenical movement of today is built on this limited humanistic basis. Working as they are for organizational union without any emphasis on spiritual unity, it is no wonder they say it makes no difference what you believe just so you follow this path of human ideals.

Lukewarmness Today

Then also it is tragic to find in our orthodox or fundamental circles those who are sound in doctrine but who are not particular about their spiritual lives. They may be faithful in attending the services and may take quite an active part in the church program, and yet not really be hot for the Lord, not all out in winning souls.

Perhaps you are a stickler for orthodoxy but only warm in your godliness. Your life doesn't show love. You fall easily into the trap of criticizing the other person because he does not believe identically the way you do. You have criticism but no compassion in your heart for others. This is lukewarmness and God will not have it.

Some of us may be convinced of the proper claims of Christianity but never make a genuine surrender of ourselves to the Lord. Does He have our lives? Does He have our pocketbooks? Does He have our time? Is He the Lord of our bodies? Is He just a convenient someone for us to come to in trouble, or have we really come to Him for salvation?

Remember that the warning is that Christ could come today and such as we have been describing He says He will spew out of His mouth. This is a very serious matter. The teaching of the Book of the Revelation is not to be used for spectacular subjects or for speculation with regard to the future. It is a very practical Book and has something for us. The Everlasting One sees through everything and nothing is hid from Him.

Let us do something about surrender and not keep putting it off. Do not be divided between living for God and for self, giving part allegiance to the Lord and part to mammon. The Lord has a job for us to do and we must be "hot" in our spiritual lives to carry it through. Genuine warmth is neutralized by coldness. The materialism of the present day has not only taken over the hearts of apostates, but it is affecting Bible-believing people too.

Some may claim to be evangelical but not evangelistic. They don't believe in mass evangelism. Let me say frankly, it is impossible to be truly evangelical in the biblical sense and not believe in evangelism. If a man is truly evangelical in this sense, he believes in hell. He believes that man is doomed and dying and needs Christ. He believes man's only escape is in Christ and it is man's responsibility to receive Christ.

An infidel lecturer once said, "If I believed what you Christians believe I would never rest day or night in my desire to tell men about it." Are we just warm enough to be born again, to be church members, but have never been convicted of the sin of omission with regard to our daily devotional lives? It would be no wonder, in that case, if soul winning and many of these other matters were lukewarm in us.

Lukewarmness in Doctrine

Spiritual lukewarmness is a condition in which conviction does not affect the conscience or the heart or the will. Many persons today in our churches are saying, "What difference does it make if Jesus is virgin-born? What difference does it make if He is coming again? We don't have to believe all these things to be Christians." The truth is that these matters are vital. If Jesus is not virgin-born He is not the Eternal God. If He is not the Eternal God He cannot be my Saviour. There are those even in fundamental circles who believe all that is vital is that Jesus Christ is Saviour. Beyond that no doctrine seems to be of any great consequence to them. But there is more to Christianity than that, and these great truths should so take hold upon us that they do something for our activity. If our convictions are not strong enough to act as springboards for our conduct, then we are lukewarm.

Some persons do not deny the fact of the cross, but it is not vital to them. Some wear it as a symbol around their necks but that is about all it means to them. This is far from being crucified with Christ which the Scriptures tell us we are if we are trusting Him.

There is more to the cross than just the fact that our Lord died upon it. To some He died as a martyr. To others He died as a Substitute and Saviour. This latter is, of course, correct, but there is even more to it than this. Paul stated it to the Galatians: "I am crucified with Christ." He was speaking of Christ as our life, the fact that we have died with Him and are now alive with Him. This is a truth that needs to grip many believers' hearts. Has it yours?

Make these things real today. Do not conduct yourself so that you hear the Lord Jesus Christ saying you are a lukewarm Christian.

There are those who admit the fact of sin. However, they don't hate it. It is not until we begin to hate sin as God hates sin that we turn from it. We say a sinner is to be pitied, but there is no real effort on the part of most Christians today to win souls to Christ. It doesn't mean anything to so many believers that a soul not trusting in Christ will be tormented in hell for eternity. When the Lord comes He will take you with Him because you trust Him, but what will happen to that person who is sitting next to you in church who is not a believer?

What about our neighbors or persons we are working with? Does their spiritual welfare not mean anything to us at all? If so, then our Christianity is lukewarm. You may have salvation yourself so that you have a ticket to heaven, a sort of an insurance policy against the lake of fire, but that may be as far as your concern goes.

We must wake up. Our Lord may come today, then what will happen to those on this earth?

Sin may be objectionable to some people, but to many Christians it is not reckoned as something rotten and poisonous that brings down the wrath of God.

It is easy also for people to be lukewarm in their creeds. They do not want to appear cold with regard to these things; at the same time to be "hot" for the Lord is looked upon by them as being undesirable excess. Thus lukewarmness is the worst kind of state to be in. A man who is cold spiritually, as we have indicated, may be won for the Lord. And there are eternal values in being hot for spiritual things. But one who is in-between is spiritually nauseating. They tell us that near the city of Laodicea were some springs of hot mineral water. It could be drunk when it was hot or quite cold, but when it was lukewarm it was nauseating. These first-century Christians knew what the Lord was referring to about being lukewarm, and we have no excuse for not knowing the same.

The Lukewarm Almost Unreachable

Saul of Tarsus was a great sinner but he was honest in his wrong thinking and doing. He thought he was doing the right thing even when he was spiritually very cold. He was in a spiritual condition in which he could be brought to the place of real life when the Lord Jesus Christ revealed Himself to him. But a man who feels himself virtuous and warm and good is hard to awaken to the realities of sin and the need of salvation. It is extremely difficult to reach such a person for Christ. He resents any suggestions that he needs to repent or to be regenerated. Anyone misses the mark who thinks faithfulness to the Lord is exclusively a matter of regular church attendance and the giving of financial gifts. There are many degrees between hot and cold and undoubtedly every Christian at one time or another passes through them from cold to hot and back again. To stop in the middle, however, is a terrible condition. There is more hope for the salvation of an atheist than for a spoiled, half-hearted, conceited and self-deceived religionist. The tax gatherer and the harlot could be more readily brought to the knowledge of Jesus Christ in the days of Christ's ministry than the santimonious Pharisees.

The lukewarm will not respond easily to the knowledge of the terrors of the Lord in judgment. Yet unless there is revival of a genuine nature among God's people, something is going to happen of a serious nature in the Western world if the Lord tarries long.

Many of us are inclined to settle down to a self-satisfied feeling that all is going well, for we read that 50 percent of the American people belong to a church. This gives some a feeling of complacency, but a complacency that produces lukewarmness.

It is not unusual for me as I am preparing messages to fall before the Lord and say, "Lord, I can say these words, but they are no good in themselves. They mean nothing unless You can use them to pierce the hearts of people to respond to Your Word and will."

The Bible warns that the Evil One can blind us to spiritual things. He can work on us to the point where we do not want to hear what God has to say. If he can keep us from awakening to our real dangers he will do so, for if we really begin to understand we will awaken fully. Unless we do awaken the Lord says He will spew us out of His mouth.

The Appeal

Our Lord's compassion revealed to Laodicea is stated in this well-known verse: "Behold, I stand at the door, and knock: if any man hear my voice, and open the door, I will come in to him, and will sup with him, and he with me" (Rev. 3:20). He is compassionate and longsuffering, for He waits. He is waiting for us to do something about it.

The picture presented is that of the Saviour standing outside the church and knocking to get in. He is standing outside of the locked heart of some person asking for entrance. Will this not in itself burden us to pray for those we know who are away from Christ? Christ does not ignore anyone, even if that person is lukewarm. Dare we ignore the spiritual condition of many around us?

Contrasting Views

The Laodiceans claimed to be rich and increased with goods and to have need of nothing. This is the condition the church thinks it is in today. It is rich in material things, a statement which describes many churches especially in North America. But many of them are minus the heavenly treasures. The church buildings are occupied with bodies rather than with souls. And those who attend are more concerned about what they wear and how they look than how they appear to God. We find today many who are concentrating on man's social needs but utterly ignoring man's spiritual needs.

What about bringing Christ to such? We may try to brush this off by saying that we are not preachers, but we are all called to the ministry of witnessing. We distinguish between what we call full-time Christian workers and others. A man who is a full-time preacher we call a "minister." Yet our Lord calls all the saints of God "ministers." Every born-again child of His is to be a witness: "Ye shall receive power, after that the Holy Ghost is come upon you: and ye shall be witnesses unto me both in Jerusalem, and in all Judaea, and in Samaria, and unto the uttermost part of the earth" (Acts 1:8).

The Laodicean church was occupied with material, earthly and temporal things rather than the spiritual, heavenly and eternal verities of God. And so it is in the Laodicean element today. It is self-centered, self-occupied, self-satisfied, self-sufficient, and over-confident. Laodicea became proud and boastful. Does this describe us today?

We have beautiful buildings, sometimes with high lofty towers and melodious chimes. We spend millions to add these things to buildings but let souls go to hell. So many care for nothing else as long as they have a nice place to meet perhaps once a week for so-called worship.

There is nothing wrong in having good buildings in which to worship God. The temple that Solomon built was a beautiful building, but it was also functional in that it was the place to meet God. Unless this is the case with us, our churches are nothing but stones and mortar. Such a church is spiritually impoverished. It has missed its spiritual enrichment and satisfaction which are found only in Christ Jesus. But Laodicea of old as Laodicea of today had spiritual blindness and did not realize its miserable condition.

Spiritually Unaware

Have we become so deaf that we cannot hear God speaking to us anymore? If so, we are in need of His mercy and salvation much more than we realize. The Laodicean church is the unbelieving church, unaffected by God's biblical truths. Because of this it is insensitive to its own need of deliverance from the dangerous impending judgments that are just ahead. There is an awareness in the world of coming judgments, perhaps as never before, yet how many realize these will be judgments from God and not just man against man? From the fourth chapter on in the Book of the Revelation we have as the main subject the final judgment of Jesus Christ upon the unsaved in the world. This will include the great religious systems that have been so unresponsive to the dealing of God in these days. Yet so many, even those who claim to be believers, are not concerned. They think it can't happen here, but God said it will.

Those in the Laodicean church considered themselves to be rich. They thought they possessed everything. Their security lay in their riches so they forgot God. Solomon prayed that he might not forget God by reason either of poverty or riches. Yet it was when his riches increased that he began to spiritually decline.

The Laodiceans were satisfied that they had need of nothing, not even anything from God. They were independent of divine help according to their own evaluation of the situation, but that was not their real condition.

According to what our Saviour said in John 15:5, we are utterly helpless without Him: "I am the vine, ye are the branches: He that abideth in me, and I in him, the same bringeth forth much fruit: for without me ye can do nothing." It is only as we are in Christ Jesus that we have anything and can be what we should be.

The lukewarmness of Laodicea made it indifferent to self-examination. This is true also of present-day Laodiceans, and such neglect can be fatal.

At Back to the Bible we constantly remind ourselves that every person writing us is an individual soul and may be in deep need of spiritual help. It is also a cause for rejoicing that the Lord has placed us in such a situation that we have to depend on Him for our day-by-day needs. We have never had riches. There has never been plenty. This has been a help to us, not a hindrance.

The Laodicean church does not think of need for spiritual power, for missionary work or for deeper life conferences. But this is symptomatic of a man freezing to death. There comes a time when he begins to feel warm again and sleepy. His condition is one thing, what he thinks of his condition is another. He doesn't realize that unless he is awakened and made to be active in order to get his blood circulating that he will die in a short time. This was Laodicea of the first century, and this is Laodicea of today.

Five Descriptive Words

The Lord Jesus said concerning the Laodiceans, "Thou art wretched, and miserable, and poor, and blind, and naked." This was His evaluation of the church as to its spiritual condition. Viewing it from eternity's standpoint, this church had nothing that a church should have. And possibly the worst factor of all was that this church knew nothing of its real condition.

Wretched

To be "wretched" means to be "oppressed" with a problem or burden. Who does not have such oppressions or burdens? Yet here was a church boasting of its wealth and its place in the world, but so spiritually helpless that it was not lifting those with burdens but was hindering and degrading them. Their wealth was actually a burden to them and they did not know it. Usually men consider death a burden, but wealth? that seems strange. But it was a burden to them because it kept them from the real thing. They lacked discernment of the true condition of their own hearts and souls. How well this fits men and women today.

Miserable

The Laodiceans were also "miserable." This means "pitiable," or "that which is in need of pity." Our Lord was moved with pity for this particular church. And it is upon individuals who reflect this same characteristic that He is moved with pity now.

Poor

Christ also said the Laodiceans were "poor." It must have shocked the members of that early church to be called "poor," for this is a word which has to do with a pauper who begs. They thought they had plenty, but Christ said they had nothing.

The same is true today. There are those who are satisfied with their affluence and yet they are in the position of beggars, needing that something that satisfies the inner heart. No one will take his wealth from this world with him. He may enjoy it for a season, but then will regret for eternity that he did not take time to place emphasis on the treasures that count. The Bible tells us of the rich man who had everything this world had to offer, but he had not taken time for his soul. The Laodicean is characterized by the lack of desire to care for himself or others in a spiritual way.

Blind

The Lord says that this was a "blind" church. They saw nothing clearly. They were nearsighted in the sense that they saw only earthly things. They had no heavenly vision. They had no grasp of what there is beyond this life. They perhaps hoped, as people are hoping today, that everything would be all right on the other side of death, but they did not know.

They lacked real spiritual vision because they lacked spiritual life. Furthermore, they had no real sense of spiritual distance. Many people are so broad-minded today that they cannot see to do anything except what is confined within their own narrow limits of knowledge and prejudice. They do not accept the broad-mindedness of Jesus Christ where He makes Himself available to everyone. "Blind leaders of the blind" is the way the Lord described them and, sad to say, many church leaders fit this category.

Being blind they lacked discernment. They could not evaluate things properly in the light of heaven and eternity. Heaven has to do with spiritual values, while the riches that men go after here are only material and cannot gain one thing for heaven so far as salvation is concerned.

Naked

The Lord added a final characteristic by saying the Laodiceans were "naked." They were nude, stripped of all clothing. The question, of course, is what kind of clothing was involved? We have touched on this before but it needs to be emphasized here also. The clothing needed will be the robe of the glory of Jesus Christ referred to as a "cloak of righteousness" so that we are fit to stand in His presence. The Book of Genesis tells us how Adam and Eve sinned and their eyes were opened and they knew they were naked. They sewed fig leaves together and made themselves aprons because they wanted to cover their shame. People are trying to do the same today, but the covering of our devising is still only spiritual nakedness. We cannot make our own garments of white raiment or cloaks of righteousness that will make us fit to stand in His presence. That comes from Christ alone when we trust Him.

Provision Through Christ

At the same time, Christ's attitude toward these who were so far from the truth was not one of ostracism but of love. He said, "I counsel thee to buy of me gold tried in the fire, that thou mayest be rich; and white raiment, that thou mayest be clothed, and that the shame of thy nakedness do not appear; and anoint thine eyes with eyesalve, that thou mayest see" (3:18).

The Lord Jesus pointed up the true danger faced by those in the Laodicean church. There was no satisfaction in their condition, but He gave the spiritual prescription, the necessary steps, that were to be taken if they wanted their real spiritual eyes to be opened. He does not pronounce judgment before first offering a way of escape. With Christ there is mercy before judgment.

We need to take stock of our heavenly treasury. There is more hope for the man who is outside of the church in spiritual coldness than for one who is inside the church lacking spiritual life, yet not aware of that lack.

Yet we can still hold out hope. The blow has not yet fallen. While the day of judgment is coming it has not yet fallen, so to all who are lost Christ makes a personal appeal saying that He stands at the door and knocks, seeking admission.

He counsels such to buy of Him gold tried in the fire. He approaches the truth of the reception of life through Christ in this language in order to carry their thoughts from their material wealth over to the spiritual wealth He alone can offer. No man can actually buy life from Christ. We are not purchased with silver and gold. But there is spiritual value in what He will provide and that will bring complete satisfaction.

To receive Christ's salvation, which is offered absolutely free, does in a sense cost the sinner something. What we mean by this is that in receiving Christ we must renounce self-righteousness. In place of being self-sufficient we must turn to His sufficiency. We boast so much of our being self-made and put up guards of self-righteousness, so for this reason the old self pays a tremendous price. It is also the price of repentance toward God and faith toward our Lord Jesus Christ, believing and trusting that He died for our sin. We no longer think of ourselves and want nothing for ourselves, but our minds and hearts are centered in Him.

I have talked to many people who say they will not take anything from charity. However, this is something we cannot have any other way than from God's heart of love. This is not something we can buy with something we have. Isaiah says, "Ho, every one that thirsteth, come ye to the waters, and he that hath no money; come ye, buy, and eat; yea, come, buy wine and milk without money and without price" (55:1).

The Lord says that we are to receive of Him gold that has been tried in the fire. This is pure gold of the highest quality. Of course the intention here is to tell us of the quality of character produced only by the indwelling Christ. The Lord invites all who are lost to receive from Him white raiment. The white raiment speaks of righteousness, a righteousness which is Christ Himself. Adam and Eve in the Garden needed to be clothed with a garment other than the ones they made. This is true of all. The garment God gives us is a cloak of righteousness, a spiritual one to cover our spiritual nakedness and to replace our self-righteous garment. Concerning this Job said, "I put on righteousness, and it clothed me: my judgment was as a robe and a diadem" (29:14).

Eye salve is needed for the eyes. The Laodiceans were

blind. Only the salve that God gives can bring sight. This is spiritual sight which we by nature do not have, for it comes only by the Holy Spirit when we are saved by repentance toward God and through trusting in Christ. The natural man does not see the things of the Spirit of God. Paul said concerning this, "But if our gospel be hid, it is hid to them that are lost: In whom the god of this world hath blinded the minds of them which believe not, lest the light of the glorious gospel of Christ, who is the image of God, should shine unto them" (II Cor. 4:3,4).

The method of removing the blindness from other men's eyes as far as we who are trusting Christ are concerned is given in I Timothy 2:1-4: "I exhort therefore, that, first of all, supplications, prayers, intercessions, and giving of thanks, be made for all men; For kings, and for all that are in authority; that we may lead a quiet and peaceable life in all godliness and honesty. For this is good and acceptable in the sight of God our Saviour; Who will have all men to be saved, and to come unto the knowledge of the truth."

So as Peter says, God is "not slack concerning His promise, as some men count slackness; but is longsuffering to us-ward, not willing that any should perish, but that all should come to repentance" (II Pet. 3:9).

Final Appeal

To the church at Laodicea and to those who are like it apart from Christ, a final appeal is given in these words: "Behold, I stand at the door, and knock: if any man hear my voice, and open the door, I will come in to him, and will sup with him, and he with me" (3:20). We are told in John 1:11-13: "He came unto his own, and his own received him not. But as many as received him, to them gave he power to become the sons of God, even to them that believe on his name: Which were born, not of blood, nor of the will of the flesh, nor of the will of man, but of God." Isaiah has this to say on the same theme: "For thus saith the high and lofty One that inhabiteth eternity, whose name is Holy; I dwell in the high and holy place, with him also that is of a contrite and humble spirit, to revive the spirit of the humble, and to revive the heart of the contrite ones" (57:15).

Even though God dwells in the highest heaven He still seeks entrance into the hearts of men. What a wonderful thing to hear Him say, "Behold, I stand at the door, and knock." Though outside the heart of the unbeliever, He is *near* offering salvation. He will never force Himself on any man, but He will plead with him. Then when such a person does open his heart, he receives the assurance from the Lord Himself: "Verily, verily, I say unto you, He that heareth my word, and believeth on him that sent me, hath everlasting life, and shall not come into condemnation; but is passed from death unto life" (John 5:24).

In the church of today, so clearly pictured prophetically in the Laodicean church of the first century, there is still the opportunity for individuals to be saved. The hierarchy in many groups have denied Christ's first coming, His deity, His virgin birth, His atonement, His bodily resurrection and Second Coming. Yet He stands outside still knocking, seeking entrance to the individual heart. How is it with you who read these words? Have you repented toward God? Is Christ in your heart? If not, will you let Him in now? There is no other way of salvation. His method is the same for all. You can do it this very minute. *So do it now.*

> Knocking, knocking, who is there?
> Waiting, waiting, oh, how fair!
> 'Tis a Pilgrim, strange and kingly,
> Never such was seen before;
> Ah! my soul, for such a wonder
> Wilt thou not undo the door?
>
> Knocking, knocking,—what! still there?
> Waiting, waiting, grand and fair;
> Yes, the pierced hand still knocketh,
> And beneath the crowned hair
> Beam the patient eyes, so tender,
> Of thy Saviour, waiting there.

Chapter Twelve

The Overcomers
(Rev. 2:7,11,17,26-28; 3:5,12,21)

At the end of each one of these letters to the seven churches there is a brief statement concerning the "overcomer." These have only been touched on lightly in a few places for we wish to consider the whole subject of the overcomer in this chapter. The word translated "overcomer" means "conqueror." The overcomer subdues, defeats and may even crush his enemy. This, of course, envisions such things for the Christian as a battle against Satan or the running of the Christian race. It is a spiritual warfare that we as Christians should participate in, and when we do, certain promises are made to us and victory is assured.

Christ the Overcomer

That Christ is an overcomer is clear from Revelation 3:21: "To him that overcometh will I grant to sit with me in my throne, even as I also overcame, and am set down with my Father in his throne." The short phrase, "as I also overcame" is the evidence for saying that He is an overcomer.

According to John 16:33 the Lord Jesus overcame the world. Here is what He said, "These things I have spoken unto you, that in me ye might have peace. In the world ye shall have tribulation; but be of good cheer; I have overcome the world." The world is ever an enemy to the Christian for the world spoken of here is the world system in which men's systems and ideas are antagonistic toward the God of the Bible.

198

Christ also overcame Satan according to Hebrews 2:14,15: "Forasmuch then as the children are partakers of flesh and blood, he also himself likewise took part of the same; that through death he might destroy him that had the power of death, that is, the devil; And deliver them who through fear of death were all their lifetime subject to bondage." This is not merely a future overcoming of Satan. It is a past overcoming that carries on through the present and into eternity. The word translated "destroy" in this passage means to "annul" or "bring to nothing." Thus, in the name of Christ we too can stand as overcomers with no reason to fear Satan or death.

There is nothing in the universe that Christ has not overcome. In his prayer that believers might be filled with knowledge and power, Paul said concerning Christ, "Which he wrought in Christ, when he raised him from the dead, and set him at his own right hand in the heavenly places, Far above all principality, and power, and might, and dominion, and every name that is named, not only in this world, but also in that which is to come: And hath put all things under his feet, and gave him to be the head over all things to the church, Which is his body, the fulness of him that filleth all in all" (Eph. 1:20-23). Do not overlook the implications with regard to the overcoming of the Church in the last portion of this quotation. Christ is the Head of the Church and He works through the Church, which is His Body, in order to fulfill His will in certain areas.

This same truth is again presented by Paul in Colossians 2:15: "And having spoiled principalities and powers, he made a shew of them openly, triumphing over them in it." There can be no doubt, then, that Christ is the Overcomer. He is the victorious One and has set the pattern for His people to follow, as well as the power to perform.

The Christian an Overcomer

The believer in the Lord is also to overcome, but his overcoming is in Christ. The moment any of us trust in Christ we are potential overcomers in the battle against sin and unrighteousness in our own hearts and in the world. According to Colossians 1:13 Christ "hath delivered us from the power of darkness, and hath translated us into the kingdom of his dear Son." This is something already done for us, not something future though it has its future benefits. We have been taken out of one kingdom, a kingdom of darkness, and placed into the kingdom of Christ. We know from what the Bible teaches that righteousness will reign on the earth during Christ's millennial reign; the glorious fact given to us here is that we are already in Christ's kingdom.

The above truth is further supported by Philippians 1:6 where the Apostle says, "Being confident of this very thing, that he which hath begun a good work in you will perform it until the day of Jesus Christ." The Lord began a work in us when we trusted in Christ and He guarantees to finish it. He is not speaking here of the ministry or work He might do through us, nor of the help some spiritual leaders or a radio testimony such as Back to the Bible might do. This is God's work in our hearts which He will perform continually until the day Christ comes for us.

We have been reconciled to God by Christ "in the body of his flesh through death, to present you holy and unblameable and unreproveable in his sight" (Col. 1:22). Then these significant words are added: "If ye continue in the faith grounded and settled." This is not referring to continuing in the faith in order to keep saved. The matter under consideration is our continuing in faith for Christian living. It is by faith we overcome in our daily walk.

Now this is not something that gives us a mere ideal but something to which we can attain because we have Christ in us, the hope of glory (Col. 1:27).

Paul goes on to say in this connection that he preaches Christ and warns every man and teaches every man in all wisdom that he may present every man perfect in Christ Jesus. The Apostle is speaking here of believers and of his work as a minister among them in order to fulfill the plans and purposes of God in perfecting each one in Christ. Then

Paul adds, "Whereunto I also labour, striving according to his working, which worketh in me mightily" (v. 29). This is the secret. There is a mighty working of the Lord in each one of us which provides the potential for our becoming overcomers in our daily walk.

We have a great enemy in the self-life and also in the world. Then back of the world is the Devil who is far more powerful than we are. Nevertheless, there is nothing for us to fear for we have everything needed to be victorious in any area of our spiritual warfare. This is strongly emphasized by the Apostle John in his First Letter: "Ye are of God, little children, and have overcome them: because greater is he that is in you, than he that is in the world" (4:4).

Method of Overcoming

First John 5:4,5 makes abundantly clear what the method of overcoming is: "For whatsoever is born of God overcometh the world: and this is the victory that overcometh the world, even our faith. Who is he that overcometh the world, but he that believeth that Jesus is the Son of God?" Faith is the key to the overcoming life. The potential is laid in our hearts the moment we trust in Christ, and it is the purpose of God that we should go on from triumph to triumph in our daily walk.

Yet we must ever remember that all we have that pleases God and everything we do that brings joy to His heart can be traced back to Christ and what He has done for us. In Romans 8, the great Epistle of salvation, we see how fully the Scriptures state the truth that all we have and are depends on Christ, including our eternity with Him. "In face of all this, what is there left to say? If God is for us, who can be against us? He who did not grudge his own Son but gave him up for us all—can we not trust such a God to give us, with him, everything else that we can need? Who would dare to accuse us, whom God has chosen? The judge himself has declared us free from sin. Who is in a position to condemn? Only Christ, and Christ died for us, Christ rose for us, Christ reigns in power for us, Christ prays for us! Who can separate us from the love of Christ? Can trouble, pain or persecution? Can lack of clothes and food, danger to life and limb, the threat of force of arms? Indeed some of us know the truth of that ancient text: "For thy sake we are killed all the day long; We were accounted as sheep for the slaughter. No, in all these things we win an overwhelming victory through him who has proved his love for us. I have become absolutely convinced that neither death nor life, neither messenger of Heaven nor monarch of earth, neither what happens today nor what may happen tomorrow, neither a power from on high nor a power from below, nor anything else in God's whole world has any power to separate us from the love of God in Christ Jesus our Lord!" (Rom. 8:31-39, *Phillips*).

The fact that overcoming is made practical through faith is presented by Paul in Colossians 2. He told the believers in Colosse that though he was absent in body he was, nevertheless, with them in spirit, rejoicing in their steadfast faith in Christ. Then he admonished them in these words: "As ye have therefore received Christ Jesus the Lord, so walk ye in him" (v. 6). Note the words "as" and "so." How do we receive Him? By faith! This is the way we appropriate Christ. So then, as we receive Christ by faith, the same faith principle is to be operative throughout our lives. We are to go ahead and walk in Christ, rooted and built up in Him and established in the faith as we have been taught. An added thought is given in Romans 8:13 where Paul says, "But if ye through the Spirit do mortify the deeds of the body, ye shall live." We have all the practical power needed in this wonderful salvation Christ provided. With the Spirit of God dwelling in us there is no need and no excuse to fail in obtaining God's objective in us.

Later on in the Book of the Revelation we will see another aspect of this same truth. In chapter 12 we learn: "And they overcame him by the blood of the Lamb, and by the word of their testimony; and they loved not their lives unto the death" (v. 11). First we learn that the blood of Christ has overcome Satan, and as we appropriate His Word (not only quote it but believe, trust and apply it), it will become a reality in us. The verse goes on to say that they loved not their lives unto death, which apparently means they wholeheartedly surrendered themselves to Him even unto death if necessary so that He might finish His work in them. This is a continuing process of faith so that failure to exercise faith on our part actually becomes sin: "For whatsoever is not of faith is sin" (Rom. 14:23).

According to I John 5:11, eternal life is in the Son. Therefore, if a person shows no practical will or determination to overcome, he is either completely blinded to his potential or he is not born again. We can say this with firmness because it is God who works in us both to will and to work according to His good pleasure.

Rewards for the Overcomer

"Blessed is he that overcometh" indicates that God places special value on this one called "overcomer." First of all, the overcomer is one who is born again and has overcome sin from the standpoint of guilt and condemnation. This great fact should in itself give us a special concern about our salvation. We should be sure we are saved—and we can know this—and then go on from there.

There are also rewards for exercising the overcoming faith. We read in Romans 8:37: "Nay, in all these things we are more than conquerors through him that loved us." We are not merely conquerors but "more than conquerors." We are conquerors in the sense that we have overcome the awfulness of eternal spiritual death through being forgiven of our sins by Jesus Christ. We are more than conquerors when we allow Christ to live in us so that we can spoil the Enemy and enjoy the throne rights spoken of in Revelation 3:21: "To him that overcometh will I grant to sit with me in my throne, even as I also overcame, and am set down with my Father in his throne."

No doubt there will be positions assigned to each child of God based on that person's faithfulness, which really means exercising *full faith.* Various scriptures point this out. To the Disciples the Lord made the promise in Matthew 19 that they would sit upon 12 thrones judging the 12 tribes of Israel because of their faithfulness.

In the parable of the pounds in Luke 19:11-27, Christ promises His faithful servants (which fact applies to those born again during this age) that they would be rulers over certain cities because of their faithfulness. There are a number of passages in the Pauline Epistles which teach this same truth. One of these is II Timothy 2:12: "If we suffer, we shall also reign with him."

The Tree of Life

Another reward having to do with the overcomer is in Revelation 2:7. He will be given by Christ fruit to eat from the tree of life which is in the midst of the Paradise of God. Our first parents, Adam and Eve, were driven out of Eden, the first Paradise. The Lord now promises a new Paradise (where no sin can enter) for the children of God, and they shall live with Him eternally and have access to the tree of life.

No Second Death

In Revelation 2:11 a promise is made that is very fitting with the circumstances surrounding the church in Smyrna, the one which saw ten seasons of severe persecution. The promise there is: "He that overcometh shall not be hurt of the second death." Many in that church had been martyred for the cause of Christ and it was especially comforting for the others to know that there is no second death for the overcomer.

Hidden Manna

Two additional rewards are stated in Revelation 2:17: "He that hath an ear, let him hear what the Spirit saith unto the churches; To him that overcometh will I give to eat of the hidden manna, and will give him a white stone, and in the stone a new name written, which no man knoweth saving he that receiveth it." In the Old Testament the reference to manna was to a literal food that God sent to provide nourishment for the children of Israel during their desert journey. Manna is referred to in the New Testament in a symbolic way in many passages and, undoubtedly, that is what is intended here. In the Old Testament, manna was necessary for life. In the New Testament, Christ is represented as the Manna from heaven and He is necessary for our spiritual life. This begins with our receiving Him according to John 1:12: "But as many as received him, to them gave he power to become the sons of God, even to them that believe on his name." This in the Revelation message is called "hidden manna" because it is hidden so far as the world is concerned. It is also hidden from the worldly Christian. To the Christian not fully surrendered to the Lord the Bible means nothing spiritually. It is just an historical book to many of them. It has fascinating stories and wonderful statements, but it doesn't become food for the soul. The fault is theirs for they do not appropriate it. Consequently, they do not grow.

The promise is made, however, to those who will go beyond the first phase of salvation and develop in the things of Christ that if they will take time to meditate on the Word of God and Christ Himself, they will find something for life that is hid with Christ in God—something never to be found anywhere else. When the Christian thus rejoices in the Word of God he is delighting in the hidden manna.

In the sixth chapter of John our Saviour was speaking to His disciples and a mixed multitude including the scribes and Pharisees. He said, "This is the bread which cometh down from heaven, that a man may eat thereof, and not die. I am the living bread which came down from heaven: if any man eat of this bread, he shall live for ever: and the bread that I will give is my flesh, which I will give for the life of the world" (vv. 50,51).

The Jews did not understand this. They argued among themselves saying, "How can this man give us his flesh to eat?" They had no spiritual understanding of these matters.

And what do these words mean to us? Some who are new in the Christian life would understandably be puzzled. But others might not know because they have not grown in the Lord. Yet the Lord takes these things which are hidden from the world and the worldly Christian and reveals them to those willing to receive them by the Holy Spirit's work and wisdom in the heart. In verse 57 we read: "As the living Father hath sent me, and I live by the Father: so he that eateth me, even he shall live by me." He is not speaking here of literal flesh any more than He was speaking of Himself as literal bread when He called Himself "the Bread of Life." This apparently puzzled all His hearers including His disciples. But it was this latter group that He asked, "Doth this offend you?" (v. 61). He then went on to explain in detail what He was talking about. He said it was the Holy Spirit who gave life. The physical flesh did not provide spiritual things. Finally He added, "The words that I speak unto you, they are spirit, and they are life." We are brought back again to the point made before that to the Christian, hidden manna will be provided if he meditates in His Word and opens his heart and life to Christ in order to have an overcoming life. So if we will allow Him to live in us and through us, daily presenting ourselves to Him to live in us for each day, we will be overcomers and partake of the hidden manna even here and now. The hidden manna is the spiritual food gleaned through faith from His Word.

A White Stone

A second reward mentioned in Revelation 2:17 for the overcomer is the white stone. This is a rather obscure reference in our day but it was well known in John's day. When a man was tried in a court of law and found innocent, he was given a white stone which signified two things. First of all, it was a stone of acquittal and at the same time it was a stone of approval. We will receive full approval of our Lord if we let Him live His holy life in us.

It was to this fact that Paul made reference when he said in II Corinthians 5:9, "Wherefore we labour, that, whether present or absent, we may be accepted of him." This is not a reference to the initial phase of our salvation, but rather His approval or "well done." We must all appear before the Judgment Seat of Christ to have our works as believers evaluated. The deeds done in the body must be considered as to whether they have been good or bad. God rewards us for those that He approves (I Cor. 3:13-15).

An added truth concerning the white stone is that there is a new name written on it which no man knows except the person who receives it. It is a secret perhaps kept in anticipation of a later revealing. It might even be something of the designation of our new character in Christ.

What's in a name? Let me illustrate. "Saul," which means "the big one" or "the great one," was changed to "Paul" which means "the little one." He was too big for God, but when he humbled himself God could use him. Then there was Jacob whose name means "supplanter." This was no pleasant name to carry around in life, especially after his heart was changed by God. The Lord gave him the new name, "Israel," which means "prince with God." Later on we find that the white stone will bear Christ's name. Surely this in itself would be a wonderful reward for overcoming.

Power Over Nations

In Revelation 2:26 the Lord Jesus said, "And he that overcometh, and keepeth my works unto the end, to him will I give power over the nations."

Look at this truth as the promise is made concerning Christ and His future rule: "Ask of me, and I shall give thee the heathen for thine inheritance, and the uttermost parts of the earth for thy possession. Thou shalt break them with a rod of iron; thou shalt dash them in pieces like a potter's vessel" (Ps. 2:8,9). Some of God's servants have taken these verses out of their context and applied them as promises to the missionary of the present day. Most certainly there is an application that might be made in this direction, but by direct interpretation this is a promise to Christ. Ruling the nations with a rod of iron and dashing them to pieces like a potter's vessel doesn't sound like salvation.

Very much the same language is used in the letter to Thyatira and is a promise to the members of the church who are faithful to Christ. The Lord Jesus Christ will rule over the nations with a rod of iron, and faithful members of the Church will reign with Him since they are His children, "And if children, then heirs; heirs of God, and joint-heirs with Christ; if so be that we suffer with him, that we may be also glorified together [with him]" (Rom. 8:17). So there are some things that the overcomer has in partnership with the Lord Jesus Christ.

According to Ephesians 1:20 God wrought power "in Christ, when he raised him from the dead, and set him at his own right hand in the heavenly places, far above all principality, and power, and might, and dominion, and every name that is named, not only in this world, but also in that which is to come." This same power has been exerted on our behalf: "And what is the exceeding greatness of his power to us-ward who believe, according to the working of his mighty power" (Eph. 1:19). Then in the following chapter is expressed the extent of that power on our behalf and what it has done to identify us with Christ: "Even when we were dead in sins, [God] hath quickened us together with Christ, (by grace are ye saved;) and hath raised us up together, and made us sit together in heavenly places in Christ Jesus" (Eph. 2:5,6). The believer has identification with the resurrected Christ in this present life and will have further identification with Him in the future Kingdom.

In Revelation 2:28 the overcomer is promised "the morning star." What is meant by the morning star? The Bible explains it for us in Revelation 22:16. "I Jesus have sent mine angel to testify unto you these things in the churches. I am the root and the offspring of David, and the bright and morning star." In His relationship to Israel, Christ says He is the root and the offspring of David. This speaks of His kinship as a man with David's family line. For the Church, Christ is the Bright and Morning Star.

Peter wrote in his Second Epistle: "We have also a more sure word of prophecy; whereunto ye do well that ye take heed, as unto a light that shineth in a dark place, until the day dawn, and the day star arise in your hearts" (1:19). We have a true word of prophecy and we should give heed to it. This prophecy shines as a light in a dark place. Now we are living in a very dark world. Which way are we going? What are all these terrible things around us coming to? Some men seem to think they have the answers but most of them do not. We, however, who trust in the Lord have the answer. If we walk with Him we will be as a light shining in a dark place until the day dawn and the day star arises in our hearts. This has reference to the coming of the Lord Jesus Christ for His Church.

To Israel He is not the Morning Star but the Sun of Righteousness. We read in Malachi 4:2: "But unto you that fear my name [Israel is in view here] shall the Sun of righteousness arise with healing in his wings; and ye shall go forth, and grow up as calves of the stall." To Israel, Christ will bring righteousness after the darkest hour, the Great Tribulation, this world has ever seen. In saying that the Tribulation is the darkest hour, we are speaking of it from the standpoint of the judgment and sorrow and suffering that shall come upon the earth. But the darkest hour of all was borne by Christ when He died for our sins on Calvary. Israel, as a nation, still has a dark hour ahead of her, but at the conclusion of it Christ will bring light to her, as well as light to the whole world.

To the Church, however, Christ is the Morning Star. In the early morning we can usually see a very bright star shining just before the day breaks. The bright shining of the morning star heralds the coming of the sun. What our Lord is telling us in this passage in Revelation is that the Rapture of the Church, which is the taking away of the Church from this earth, is announced by the Morning Star. He is our Morning Star and will remove us from this world of darkness before He returns as the Sun of Righteousness for Israel.

In Revelation 3:10 the church in Philadelphia is

promised: "Because thou hast kept the word of my patience, I also will keep thee from the hour of temptation, which shall come upon all the world, to try them that dwell upon the earth. Behold, I come quickly: hold that fast which thou hast, that no man take thy crown." Do you who read this know Him as your personal Saviour? His coming as the Morning Star may not be very far off. If you are trusting Him now you will go with Him then.

White Raiment

White raiment is also promised the overcomer. This is the promise in Revelation 3:5: "He that overcometh, the same shall be clothed in white raiment; and I will not blot out his name out of the book of life, but I will confess his name before my Father, and before his angels." The white raiment speaks of our being clothed with Christ who is our righteousness.

Name Not Blotted Out

Furthermore, the promise is that the Lord will not blot out our names from the Lamb's Book of Life. Instead, He will confess our names before the Heavenly Father. Remember our Lord said, "Whosoever therefore shall confess me before men, him will I confess also before my Father which is in heaven. But whosoever shall deny me before men, him will I also deny before my Father which is in heaven" (Matt. 10:32,33). Evidently the Heavenly Father will be handing out the rewards.

A Pillar in the Temple

To the overcomer in the church of Philadelphia the Lord gives these promises: "Him that overcometh will I make a pillar in the temple of my God, and he shall go no more out: and I will write upon him the name of my God, and the name of the city of my God, which is new Jerusalem, which cometh down out of heaven from my God: and I will write upon him my new name" (Rev. 3:12). The overcomer is the one who surmounts difficulties, conquers foes, subdues enemies—in short is victorious here in this life over the enemies of God and the Bible.

The promise to the overcomer of being made a pillar in the temple of God is without doubt figurative language. As someone has pointed out, in the New Jerusalem the Lord Himself will be the temple. And so the suggestion is made that in Christ the overcomers will be pillars of strength in Him. So one day we shall be found in the New Jerusalem, standing as pillars in the radiant glory of His presence which shall not only rest upon us but also shine forth from us.

Forever in His Presence

Still another comforting and encouraging promise is made that the overcomer will "go no more out" from the presence of God (3:12). What a wonderful thing to be eternally secure in Christ. No sin will be allowed in the New Heaven or the New Jerusalem or the new earth. We will be forever separated from it.

This separation from sin forever will be in direct contrast to what happened to Adam and Eve. They were first placed in the Garden of Eden where there was no sin. Then sin entered and because they took part in it, they were driven out of the Garden. But now the promise is that in that day there never will be sin again. No child of God will sin again. Thus no member of God's family will ever be deprived of the heavenly Garden. We have this glorious assurance even now according to Ephesians 1:13 where we are told that we are sealed unto the day of redemption by no less power than the Holy Spirit Himself.

A New Name

Added to all these is the fact that Christ said He would write upon the overcomer His own "new name" (3:12). This is a name that has not yet been revealed, but it will be a name of authority because Christ was given a name above all names. So this speaks of exalted position and authority and the necessary power to carry out the work of God throughout eternity.

Seated With Christ

The final great reward is promised in Revelation 3:21: "To him that overcometh will I grant to sit with me in my throne, even as I also overcame, and am set down with my Father in his throne." This has to do with throne rights, and these belong to the firstborn. Jesus is the firstborn but we are joint heirs with Him and will inherit with Him. Those who are faithful will rule with Him and He will confess them before the Father. He will make us pillars in His temple. In other words, those who stand firm for Him will have a place in His throne.

Friend, it is worth everything to let Jesus overcome in your life. Allow Him to do so and you will be an overcomer at all times for Him.